173
Pre-Prohibition
Cocktails

Potations So Good
They Scandalized
a President

Written by
Tom Bullock and D.J. Frienz

Howling at the Moon Press

Book cover and interior design © TLC Graphics, www.TLCGraphics.com
Cover illustration by Laurie Barrows, illustration copyright 2000 by Laurie Barrows

10   9   8   7   6   5   4   3   2   1

Publisher's Cataloging-in-Publication
    (provided by Quality Books, Inc.)

Bullock, Tom,1873-1964
        173 pre-Prohibition cocktails : potations
    so good they scandalized a president / written by Tom
    Bullock and D. J. Frienz. -- 1st ed.
        p. cm.
        Includes index.
        LCCN: 00-102382
        ISBN: 0-9654333-2-3

        1. Cocktails. 2. Alcoholic beverages--United
    States--History--1913-1921.   I. Frienz, D. J.
    II. Title.

    TX951.B85 2000   641.8'74
                                    QBI00-450

Howl at the moon!
Celebrate, because we are all part of each other
during this great adventure we call "life."

Howling at the Moon Press
P.O. Box 666
Jenks, OK   74037
E-mail: HATMPress@aol.com
On the World Wide Web: http://www.howling1.com

TO ORDER, CALL TOLL-FREE: 877-4-HOWLING

Printed in the U.S.A.

"Is it any wonder that mankind stands open-mouthed before the bartender, considering the mysteries and marvels of an art that borders on magic? The recipes found in this book have been composed and collected, tried and tested, in a quarter-century of experience by Tom Bullock of the St. Louis Country Club."

Excerpted from Tom Bullock's
1917 classic, *The Ideal Bartender*

A Toast

The publisher of this book would like to toast
the many people without whom this book could not have been made:

To Tom Bullock, those who loved him, and their descendants.

David Lupton, African-American cookbook bibliographer
extraordinaire, without whose dedication and commitment
Tom Bullock's recipes could not have been found.

Phenomenal bartender and Renaissance man Tom Rush, in much
appreciation of his knowledge of history, the human condition,
and the occasional libation enjoyed under his watchful and wise eyes.

Fredrick V. Wellington, Ph.D., and Julie A. Watt, M.A., J.D.,
fine editors and mixologists in their own right.

Researcher Mrs. E. Louise King of St. Louis, Michael Blechner, Ph.D.,
Elizabeth White, The State Historical Society of Missouri,
The Kentucky Historical Society, The Library of Congress,
The Schomburg Center for Research in Black Culture, and all the
genealogical webmasters who dedicate so much of their lives to
preserving and sharing the stories of those who came before us.

Tamara Dever at TLC Graphics, Alicia Stone Diehl, Jack Cullinan,
Helen Shaw, The Chicago Historical Society, The Filsom Club
of Louisville, B&O Railroad Museum, Jim Porterfield,
and Stan Mulford of Circus Train.

Special thanks to Anheuser-Busch, Mr. Jerry Borofsky of
Paradise Found, Gerry Gray, Steve Quinn of Steve Quinn
Creative Services, Kerry Walsh of Walsh Associates, Harry Bilger,
and L. B. Woods Antiques & Collectibles.

May all of you celebrate good health, enough wealth, and dear, dear
friends as long as you live. And may you live a long, long time.

PUBLISHER'S NOTE

The cocktail recipes in *173 Pre-Prohibition Cocktails* were first recorded by Tom Bullock in his 1917 book *The Ideal Bartender*.

The editors of this book have tried to retain any "imperfections" Mr. Bullock may have made. His typing errors, misspellings, or inconsistencies, we believe, memorialize the original flavor and history of the book and enhance it, just as an "imperfection" in a fine fabric enhances its texture and value.

Playing cards at the country club.

By Clarence Underwood, 1900.

Dedicated

To those who enjoy snug club rooms, that they may learn the art of preparing for themselves what is good.

From Tom Bullock's 1917 Magnum Opus,
The Ideal Bartender

Master bartender Tom Bullock's recipes first appeared
in the book he wrote and published in 1917,
The Ideal Bartender.

INTRODUCTION

I have known the author of "The Ideal Bartender" for many years, and it is a genuine privilege to be permitted to testify to his qualifications for such a work.

To his many friends in St. Louis, Louisville, Cincinnati, Chicago and elsewhere, my word will be superfluous, but to those who do not know him, and who are to be the gainers by following his advices, it may prove at the very beginning a stimulus to know something of his record of achievement.

For the past quarter of a century he has refreshed and delighted the members and their friends of the Pendennis Club of Louisville and the St. Louis Country Club of St. Louis. In all that time I doubt if he has erred in even one of his concoctions. Thus if there is "many a slip twixt the cup and the lip" it has been none of his doing, but rather the fault of those who have appreciated his art too highly. But why go on! His work is before you. It is the best to be had. Follow on, and as you sip the nectar of his schemings tell your friends, to the end that both they and he may be benefitted.

GEORGE HERBERT WALKER

(1875 to 1953)

Grandfather of 41st President of the U.S.,

George Herbert Walker Bush, and patron of the St. Louis Country Club

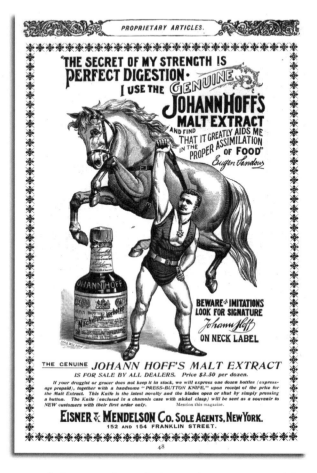

"The secret of my strength ... ," claims the strong man lifting the muscular stallion, is "I use the genuine Johann Hoff's Malt Extract."

Many people still believe malt, germinated from barley and roasted, adds nutritive value to the beer and ales distilled from it. British poet A.E. Housman (1859 - 1936) attributed a more spiritual dimension to the substance. He said, "Malt does more than Milton can to justify God's ways to man."

Advertisement from October, 1897 Chautauguan Magazine.

FOREWORD

If ever America needed a drink, it was in 1917. A flu pandemic killed almost 22 million people worldwide, the first terrible war in the darkened dawn across the Atlantic Ocean ensnared American boy after American boy, and, here at home, women in bedrooms across the country held their knees together in an effort to coerce their men into giving them the right to vote.

1917 was also the year Tom Bullock, an American of African descent, published a cocktail book he called *The Ideal Bartender*.

Mr. Bullock may have been "the ideal bartender" to the wealthy men and women he served in exclusive country clubs and aboard luxurious train cars, but his own life was less than ideal. He was born shortly after the end of the Civil War in Louisville, Kentucky, during a time when he was legally no longer a slave but into a geography of the mind where he did not yet have the same rights as other men.

After Mr. Bullock published *The Ideal Bartender*, his world became even more complicated. It became illegal for him to practice his trade for thirteen long, hard Prohibition years, the most cocktail-centered years in American history. Fortunately, many of his clients were lawyers, judges, and statesmen.

Although Mr. Bullock's life remained characterized by dichotomies until his death in 1964, his legacy remains a cocktail book that was the first written by an African-American, a Julep recipe so unforgettable even Teddy Roosevelt felt compelled to mention it under oath, and many, many thirsty friends.

Among these friends were two great men who would help shape the destiny of this country, August A. Busch, Sr. and George Herbert Walker.

August Busch was the man whose inventiveness kept thousands of people legally employed and millions more fed during thirteen long, hard, Prohibition years and the subsequent early phase of the Great Depression. Anheuser-Busch, the company his ingeniousness saved, has helped shape the face of American culture for at least 100 years.

Evidence of Tom Bullock's fondness for August Busch exists in *The Ideal Bartender*. Bevo, a non-alcoholic beer invented by Busch in 1916, is a major ingredient in a beverage recipe Mr. Bullock created and named "Golfer's Delight - Home of Bevo - 18th Hole." The recipe is included in this book.

The other significant friend mentioned in *The Ideal Bartender* is George Herbert (G.H.) Walker, best known as the founder of golf's Walker Cup and grandfather of 41st U.S. President George Herbert Walker Bush.

G. H. Walker was, perhaps, Tom Bullock's biggest fan. His signature style and grace are indelibly imprinted in *The Ideal Bartender*. For instance, the forward to *The Ideal Bartender* was openly penned by Walker and also acts as the forward to this book.

Young Theodore Roosevelt's lips (featured above)
may never have touched liquor but ...

Walker's eloquent voice, I think, also appears in an anonymous *St. Louis Dispatch* editorial from May of 1913 that deifies Tom.

At that time, former President Teddy Roosevelt was being publicly accused in several newspapers of being a drunk unfit for an office he desired. TR sued in order to reclaim a reputation as a sober and temperate man, and testified in court that he had only consumed parts of two drinks in his life: a sip of beer while campaigning at a brewery in Milwaukee and a part of a Mint Julep at the St. Louis Country Club. The editorial his testimony inspired follows:

... to believe seasoned war hero and President Teddy Roosevelt (seen here in the September 25, 1902 issue of *Leslie's Weekly* with representatives from the press) could drink only a part of a julep Tom Bullock served him at the St. Louis Country Club strained the former President's credibility too far.

"Colonel Roosevelt's fatal admission that he drank just a part of one julep at the St. Louis Country Club will come very near losing his case.

Who was ever known to drink just a part of one of Tom's? Tom, than whom there is no greater mixologist of any race, color or condition of servitude, was taught the art of the julep by no less than Marse Lilburn G. McNair, the father of the julep. In fact, the very cup that Col. Roosevelt drank it from belonged to Governor McNair, the first Governor of Missouri, the great-grandfather of Marse Lilburn and the great-great-grandfather of the julep.

As is well know, the Country Club mint originally sprang on the slopes of Parnassus and was transplanted thence to the bosky banks of Culpeper Creek, Gaines County, Ky., and thence to our own environs; while the classic distillation with which Tom mingles it to produce his chief d'oeuvre is the oft-quoted liquefied soul of a Southern moonbeam falling aslant the dewy slopes of the Cumberland Mountains.

To believe that a red-blooded man, and a true Colonel at that, ever stopped with just a part of one of those refreshments which have made St. Louis hospitality proverbial and become one of our most distinctive genre institutions, is to strain credulity too far. Are the Colonel's powers of self restraint altogether transcendent? Have we found the living superman at last?

When the Colonel says that he consumed just a part of one he doubtless meant that he did not swallow the mint itself, munch the ice and devour the very cup."

St. Louis Post-Dispatch
editorial from May 28, 1913

Regardless of the author of this editorial's strong feelings (as well as those of many Americans), Roosevelt won his libel suit and received a token sum from the editor who had accused him of drunkenness. Roosevelt's reputation as a sober man has not, however, been borne out through history.

Almost forgotten in history as well are the days when the line between the services performed by a bartender, pharmacist, and physician blurred. Yes, the importance of the bartender during the westward movement of America has all but disappeared from our collective memory, along with the specialized knowledge of combining healing herbs into restorative "tonics," soothing "seltzers," and curative potions for the suffering pioneers who lived weeks or months from any doctor.

Let us not forget, then, the amazing Tom Bullock, his delightful recipes, and his lessons of history and friendship.

Tom Bullock's Almost-Lost Recipes

In 1900, ABSINTHE was one of the few drinks American women could sip at their local coffee house and still be considered ladies. A few years later, the powerful green liquor's reputation was under siege. Some critics say the "green fairy" took Vincent Van Gogh's (1853–1890) ear, inspired French poet Paul Verlaine (1844–1896) to shoot fellow poet and lover Arthur Rimbaud (1854–1891), and caused Ernest Hemingway (1899-1961) to eventually twist a loaded shotgun into his mouth.

Illustration by Harrison Fisher, 1911.

ABRICONTINE POUSSE CAFE

Fill Pousse Cafe glass one-third full of Abricontine and add Maraschino, Curacoa, Chartreuse and Brandy in equal proportions until the glass is filled. The ingredients should be poured in one after the other from a small Wine glass, with great care, to prevent the colors from blending. Ignite the Brandy on top, and after it has blazed for a few seconds extinguish it by placing a saucer or the bottom of another glass over the blazing fluid. Then serve.

ABSINTHE

When the customer asks for Absinthe
without specifying any particular style of service.

Pour one pony of Absinthe into large Bar glass and let ice cold water drip from the Absinthe glass into Bar glass until full. The Absinthe glass has a hole in the center. By filling the bowl of the Absinthe glass partly with Shaved Ice, and the rest with water, the water will be ice cold as it drops from the Absinthe glass.

ABSINTHE, AMERICAN SERVICE

Mixing glass 3/4 full Shaved Ice.
4 dashes Gum Syrup.
1 pony Absinthe.

Shake until outside of shaker is well frosted; strain into large Champagne glass and serve.

ABSINTHE COCKTAIL

Fill Mixing glass 3/4 full Shaved Ice.
1/2 jigger Water.
1/2 jigger Absinthe.
2 dashes Angostura Bitters.
1 teaspoonful Benedictine.

Stir; strain into Cocktail glass and serve.

ABSINTHE FRAPPE

Fill medium Bar glass full of Shaved Ice.

1 teaspoonful Benedictine.

1 pony Absinthe.

Shake until outside of Shaker has frosty appearance;
strain into six-ounce Shell glass and serve.

ABSINTHE, FRENCH SERVICE

Pour 1 pony of Absinthe into a Champagne glass which is standing
in a bowl. Fill the bowl of your Absinthe glass with Shaved Ice and
water. Raise the bowl and let the Ice Water drip into the Absinthe
until the proper color is obtained. Serve in thin Bar glass.

ABSINTHE, ITALIAN SERVICE

1 pony of Absinthe in a large Bar glass.

3 pieces Cracked Ice.

3 dashes Maraschino.

1/2 pony Anisette.

Pour Ice Water in glass, at same time stirring gently with Bar
Spoon. Serve.

ADMIRAL SCHLEY HIGH BALL

Drop a piece of Ice into a High Ball glass.

1 teaspoonful Pineapple Syrup.

1 teaspoonful Lemon Juice.

2/3 jigger Irish Whiskey.

2/3 jigger Tokay, Angelica or Sweet Catawba Wine.

Fill up with Apollinaris or Seltzer.

ALE FLIP

Fill an Ale glass nearly full.
1 teaspoonful of Bar Sugar.
Break in 1 whole Egg; grate a little Nutmeg on top and
serve the drink with a spoon alongside of the glass.

ALE SANGAREE

Dissolve in an Ale glass 1 teaspoonful Bar Sugar.
Fill up with Ale and serve with grated Nutmeg on top.

ALL RIGHT COCKTAIL

Use a large Mixing glass filled with Lump Ice.
1 jigger Rye Whiskey.
2/3 jigger Orange Curacoa.
1 dash Angostura Bitters.

Shake well; strain into Cocktail glass and serve.

AMERICAN POUSSE CAFE

Fill a Pousse Cafe glass 1/4 full of Chartreuse, and add
Maraschino, Curacoa and Brandy in equal proportions until the
glass is filled. Then proceed as for Abricontine Pousse Cafe.

APOLLINARIS LEMONADE

Fill large Bar glass 2/3 full Shaved Ice.
2 teaspoonfuls Powdered Sugar.
1 Lemon's Juice.

Fill up with Apollinaris; stir; strain into Lemonade glass;
dress with Fruit and serve.

Something New.

Spring of 1895.

506

This watercolor of a woman holding a basket of lemons and a child encouraged the sale of men's suits at a sale price of $9.95.

1895 trading card by the Besse, Baker & Company's chain of 27 stores.

APPLE JACK COCKTAIL

Fill large Bar glass 3/4 full Shaved Ice.
3 dashes Gum Syrup.
3 dashes Raspberry Syrup.
1 1/4 jiggers Applejack.

Shake; strain into Cocktail glass and
serve with piece of Lemon Peel twisted on top.

APPLEJACK FIX

Fill large Bar glass with Shaved Ice.
2 teaspoonfuls Bar Sugar, dissolved in little Water.
1/4 Juice of 1 Lemon.
3 dashes of Curacoa.
4 dashes of any Fruit Syrup.
1 jigger Applejack Brandy.

Stir; dress with Fruits; serve with Straws.

APPLEJACK SOUR

Fill large Bar glass 3/4 full Shaved Ice.
2 teaspoonfuls Bar Sugar, dissolved in little Water.
3 dashes Lemon or Lime Juice.
1 jigger Applejack.

Stir well; strain into Sour glass; dress with
Fruit and Berries and serve.

"ARF-AND-ARF"

Pour into an Ale glass or mug 1/2 Porter and 1/2 Ale,
or Porter and Stout with Ale, or 1/2 Old and 1/2 New Ale.
The use of the Porter and Ale is more prevalent in England.
In the United States 1/2 Old and 1/2 New Ale is usually used
when this drink is called for, unless otherwise specified.

ARRACK PUNCH

Pour into a Punch glass the Juice of 1 Lime and a little Apollinaris
Water in which a heaping teaspoonful of Bar Sugar has been
dissolved. Add 1 Lump Ice.
3/4 jigger Batavia Arrack.
1/4 jigger Jamaica Rum.
Stir well; dash with Champagne; stir again briskly;
dress with Fruit and Serve.

ASTRINGENT

1/2 Wineglass Port Wine.
6 dashes Jamaica Ginger.

Fill up with Brandy; stir gently and
serve with little Nutmeg on top.

AUDITORIUM COOLER

Into large Bar glass squeeze Juice of 1 Lemon.
1 teaspoonful Bar Sugar.
1 bottle Ginger Ale off the ice.

Stir; decorate with Fruit and Berries. Serve.

BACARDI COCKTAIL

Use a large Mixing glass.
Fill with Lump Ice.
1/2 jigger Cusiner Grenadine.
1 jigger Bacardi Rum.

Shake well and serve in a Cocktail glass.

"Buy by the case from your grocer or druggist. Keep in pantry, and a few bottles on ice," recommends this Clicquot Ginger Ale advertisement from the August, 1918 issue of *The Ladies' Home Journal*. Refrigerators had been available for about 2 years, but most people couldn't afford them (the cost was about $900, roughly the price of an automobile).

Advertisement courtesy of Jerry Borofsky, Paradise Found Antiques, Jenks, OK

BACARDI COCKTAIL - Country Club Style

Use a large Mixing glass.
Fill with Lump Ice.
1/2 Lime Juice.
2 dashes Imported Grenadine.
1 jigger Bacardi Rum.

Shake well; strain into Cocktail glass and serve.

BALDY COCKTAIL

Use a large Mixing glass with Lump Ice.
1 jigger of Burnette's Old Tom Gin.
1 pony of Orange Juice.
1 Dash of Orange Bitters.

Shake; strain into Cocktail glass and serve.

BAMBOO COCKTAIL

Fill large Bar glass 1/3 full Fine Ice.
3/4 jigger Sherry Wine.
3/4 jigger Italian Vermouth.

Stir; strain into Cocktail glass. Serve.

BEEF TEA

1/2 teaspoonful Beef Extract in small Bar glass.
Fill glass with Hot Water. Stir well while seasoning with
Pepper, Salt and Celery Salt. Serve with small glass of
Cracked Ice and spoon on the side.

BENEDICTINE

Place an inverted Whiskey glass on the bar, set a Pony glass on it and
fill up with Benedictine. Serve all liquors straight in this manner.

BISHOP

1 teaspoonful Bar Sugar in large Bar glass.
2 dashes Lemon Juice with the Skin of Two Slices.
Fill glass 3/4 full Shaved Ice.
1 dash Seltzer Water.
2 dashes Jamaica Rum.

Fill up with Claret or Burgundy; shake;
ornament with Fruit and serve with Straws.

BISHOP A LA PRUSSE

Before a Fire or in a Hot Oven roast 6 large Oranges until they
are of a light brown color, and then place them in a deep dish and
scatter over them 1/2 lb. of Granulated Sugar and pour on 1 pint
of Port or Claret Wine. Then cover the dish and set aside for
24 hours before the time to serve. When about ready for the service,
set the dish in boiling water; press the Juice from the Oranges
with a large spoon or wooden potato masher and strain the
Juice through a fine seive or cheese cloth. Then boil 1 pint of Port
or Claret and mix it with the Strained Juice. Serve in stem Claret
glasses while warm. A little Nutmeg on top improves the drink,
but should not be added unless requested by customer or guest.

BISMARCK

2 teaspoonfuls Vanilla Cordial in Sherry Wine glass.
1 yolk of an Egg covered with Benedictine so as
not to break the yolk.
1/2 Wineglass Kuemmel.
1 light dash Angostura Bitters.

The colors should be kept separate and great care exercised
to prevent the ingredients from running together.

In 18th century France, wine and beer spoiled easily, threatening both the quality of a Frenchman's life and his economy. Chemist and biologist Louis Pasteur (1822-1895) devoted much of his life to solving the problem. His solution for preserving wine and beer was eventually used to "pasteurize" milk and cream, making both safer to drink.

Pictured above, this cream separator was one of "Thousands In Use" as advertised in the March 7, 1914 New England Homestead.

"I WISH I COULD DRINK LIKE A LADY.
I CAN TAKE ONE OR TWO AT THE MOST.
THREE AND I'M UNDER THE TABLE,
FOUR AND I'M UNDER THE HOST."

DOROTHY PARKER
(1893-1967)

BIZZY IZZY HIGH BALL

Drop 1 piece of Ice into a Highball glass.
2 dashes Lemon Juice.
2 teaspoonfuls Pineapple Syrup.
1/2 jigger Sherry Wine.
1/2 jigger Rye or Bourbon Whiskey.

BLACK AND TAN PUNCH

For party of 10

1 lb. white Sugar.
Juice of 6 Lemons.
1 quart Guinness Stout.
1 quart Champagne.

Pour into mixture of Lemon Juice and
Sugar the Champagne and Stout, ice cold.
Serve in Punch glasses dressed with Fruit.

BLACK COW

Use a large Mixing glass with Lump Ice.
2 jiggers of Cream.
1 bottle Sarsaparilla.

Stir well and serve with Straws.

BLACK STRIPE

Pour Wineglass Santa Cruz or Jamaica Rum into a
small Bar glass and add 1 tablespoonful of Molasses.
If to serve hot, fill glass with boiling Water
and sprinkle Nutmeg on top.
If to serve cold, add 1/2 Wineglass Water.
Stir well and fill up with Shaved Ice.

Tom Bullock's Black and Tan Punch and Champagne Velvet recipes are variations on what we now call a Black Velvet. Rumor has it all of England mourned in 1861, when Prince Albert died. A steward decided champagne should be in mourning too, so he mixed it with Guinness Stout. The Black Velvet, still a favorite in Great Britain, was born. Above, sailors in a 1903 *Harper's Magazine* advertisement pitch Pommery Champagne and toast, "To our sweethearts and wives."

BLACKTHORNE COCKTAIL

Fill Mixing glass 2/3 full Shaved Ice.
1/4 teaspoonful Lemon Juice.
1 teaspoonful Syrup.
1/2 jigger Vermouth.
1/2 jigger Sloe Gin.
1 dash Angostura Bitters.
2 dashes Orange Bitters.

Stir; strain into Cocktail glass and serve.

BLACKTHORNE SOUR

Fill large Bar glass 2/3 full Shaved Ice.
4 dashes Lime or Lemon Juice.
1 teaspoonful Pineapple Syrup.
1/2 teaspoonful green Chartreuse.
1 jigger Sloe Gin.

Stir; strain into Claret glass; ornament with Fruit and serve.

BLIZ'S ROYAL RICKEY

Drop 3 lumps Cracked Ice in a Rickey (thin Champagne) glass.
1/2 Lime or 1/4 Lemon.
4 dashes Raspberry Syrup.
1 pony Vermouth.
3/4 jigger Gin.

Fill up with Ginger Ale (imported); stir;
dress with Fruit and serve.

BLOOD HOUND COCKTAIL

Fill large Bar glass 1/2 full Shaved Ice.
Add 1/2 dozen fresh Strawberries.
1 jigger Burnette's Old Tom Gin.

Shake well; strain into Cocktail glass and serve.

Pyrotechnics from the 1860s! Jerry "The Professor" Thomas, still famous for writing some of the first American bar guides and inventing a classic drink called the Tom & Jerry, also created the most spectacular drink of his time, the Blue Blazer. For decades, revelers lined up to watch their favorite bartender quickly toss blue-flamed liquid from cup to cup. Here, the Vulcan Handy Alcohol cup is featured in a 1909 advertisement.

BLUE BLAZER

Use two Pewter or Silver Mugs.
1 teaspoonful Bar Sugar dissolved in a little Hot Water.
1 Wineglass (or jigger) Scotch Whiskey.

Ignite the mixture, and while blazing pour it several times from one mug to the other. Serve with a piece of twisted Lemon Peel on top.

BOATING PUNCH

Into a large Bar glass put:

2 teaspoonfuls Bar Sugar.

2 dashes Lemon Juice.

1 dash Lime Juice.

Fill up with Shaved Ice and add:

1 pony Brandy.

1 jigger Santa Cruz Rum.

Stir; dress with Fruit and serve with Straws.

BOMBAY COCKTAIL

Use a Claret glass.

1/2 pony Olive Oil.

1/2 pony Vinegar.

1/2 pony Worcestershire Sauce.

Break one Ice Cold Egg into glass.

Add salt and Spanish Paprica and serve.

BOMBAY PUNCH

2 1/2-gallon mixture for 40 people

Bruise the skins of 6 Lemons in 1 lb. of Bar sugar and
put the Sugar in a Punch bowl and add:

1 box Strawberries.

2 Lemons, sliced.

6 Oranges, sliced.

1 Pineapple, cut into small pieces.

1 quart Brandy.

1 quart Sherry Wine.

1 quart Madeira Wine.

Stir well; empty into another bowl in which a block of Clear Ice
has been placed and add:

4 quarts of Champagne.

2 quarts Carbonated Water.

Serve into Punch glasses so that each person will have some of the Fruit.

BON SOIR ("Good Night")

Fill a Sherry glass 1/2 full of Shaved Ice.

1/2 pony Benedictine.

1/2 pony Creme Yvette.

Fill up with Ginger Ale; stir gently and
serve with a Straw cut in two.

BOSTON COOLER

1 Lemon Rind in large Bar glass.

3 lumps Ice.

1 bottle Ginger Ale.

1 bottle Sarsaparilla.

Serve.

BOTTLE OF COCKTAIL

Pour a quart of Whiskey or other Liquor desired into a Bar
measure or glass pitcher and add:

1 jigger Gum Syrup.

1 pony Curacoa.

3/4 pony Angostura Bitters.

Pour back and forth from one measure or pitcher into
another measure or pitcher until the liquid is thoroughly mixed.
Bottle and cork.

BRACE UP

1 tablespoonful Bar Sugar in large Mixing glass.

3 dashes Boker's or Angostura Bitters.

3 dashes Lemon Juice.

2 dashes Anisette.

1 Egg.

1 jigger Brandy

1/2 glass Shaved Ice.

Shake well; strain into tall, thin glass; fill with Apollinaris and serve.

"ALL OF THE GREAT VILLAINIES OF THE WORLD
... HAVE BEEN PERPETUATED BY SOBER MEN,
AND CHIEFLY BY TEETOTALERS."

H. L. MENCKEN
(1880-1956)

BRANDY AND GINGER ALE

3 lumps of Ice in tall, thin glass.
1 Wineglass Brandy.
1 bottle Ginger Ale.

Stir briskly and serve.

BRANDY AND SODA

2 pieces of Ice in tall, thin glass.
1 Wineglass Brandy.
1 bottle plain Soda.

Stir briskly and serve.

BRANDY FLIP

Fill medium Bar glass 1/4 full Shaved Ice.
1 Egg broken in whole.
2 level teaspoonfuls Bar Sugar.
1 jigger Brandy.

Shake well; strain into small Shell glass;
grate a little Nutmeg on top and serve.

BRANDY FLOAT

Fill a Cocktail glass 2/3 full of Carbonated Water.
1 pony Brandy floated on top. (Use spoon to float the Brandy).

BRANDY JULEP

Into a small Bar glass pour 3/4 Wineglass of Water and stir in
1 heaping teaspoonful of Bar Sugar. Bruise 3 or 4 sprigs of Mint
in the Sugar and Water with a Muddler until the flavor of the
Mint has been extracted. Then withdraw the Mint and pour the
flavored Water into a tall Shell glass or large Goblet,
which has been filled with fine Ice, and add:

1 jigger of Brandy.

2 dashes Jamaica Rum.

Stir well; decorate with few sprigs of Mint by planting the sprigs
stems downward in the Ice around the rim of glass;
dress with Fruit and serve.

BRANDY PUNCH

Fill large Bar glass 3/4 full Shaved Ice.

2 teaspoonfuls Bar Sugar dissolved in little Water.

1/2 Juice of 1 Lemon.

1/4 jigger Santa Cruz Rum.

1 1/2 jiggers Brandy.

1 slice Orange.

1 piece of Pineapple.

Shake; dress with Fruit and serve with Straw.

BRANDY SCAFFA

Into a small Wineglass pour:

Green Chartreuse.

Maraschino.

Old Brandy.

In equal proportion to fill the glass, using care as in
preparing Crustas, not to allow the colors to blend.

Would you kick someone out of the country who made a liqueur this amazing? Surprisingly, the French government did in 1903 when it made the Carthusian monks, a contemplative order founded during the 11th century, leave. The French thought again and let the monks and their "La Grande Chartreuse" liquid come home in 1941.

Green Chartreuse is more readily available, has a slightly higher alcohol content, and is more flavorful than yellow Chartreuse. Some say the green hue comes from chlorophyll. The yellow variety is sweeter, milder, and more aromatic, perhaps receiving its color from a touch of saffron. Both varieties have 130 herbs and spices and are aged in oak.

Red Book Magazine advertisement, 1903.

BRANDY SHAKE

Fill small Bar glass 3/4 full Shaved Ice.

1 teaspoonful Bar Sugar.

Juice of 2 Limes.

1 jigger Brandy.

Shake; strain into small fancy glass and serve.

BRANDY SHRUB

2-gallon mixture for 40 people

Into a Punch bowl put the Peeled Rinds of 5 Lemons and the Juice of 12 Lemons and add 5 quarts of Brandy. Make the bowl airtight and set it aside. At the expiration of 6 days add 3 quarts of Sherry wine and 6 pounds of Loaf Sugar, which has been dissolved in 1 quart of plain Soda. Strain through a bag and bottle.

BRANDY SKIN

Fill a Whiskey glass 1/2 full Hot Water and pour in:
1 jigger Brandy.
Twist a piece of Lemon Skin on top and serve.
(It may occur that a customer will ask for a little Sugar.
In that case add 1/2 small teaspoonful, and stir).

BRANDY SLING

In a Whiskey glass:
1 lump Ice.
1 teaspoonful Sugar dissolved in little Water.
1 jigger Brandy.

Stir; twist in a piece of Lemon Peel;
grate Nutmeg on top and serve.

BRANDY SMASH

Fill large Bar glass 1/2 full Shaved Ice.
1 heaping teaspoonful Bar Sugar.
3 sprigs of Mint.
1 jigger Brandy.

Stir; strain into fancy Stem glass and serve.

BRANDY SOUR

Fill large Bar glass 3/4 full Shaved Ice.
2 teaspoonfuls Bar Sugar.
3 dashes Lemon or Lime Juice.
3 dashes Seltzer or Apollinaris Water.
1 jigger Brandy.

Stir; strain into Sour glass; dress with Fruit and serve.

BRANDY TODDY

Into a Whiskey glass drop 1 lump Cracked Ice.
1 teaspoonful of Bar Sugar dissolved in little Water.

Stir; place the bottle before the customer and
allow him to pour his own drink.

BRONX COCKTAIL

Fill large Bar glass 3/4 full Shaved Ice.
1/3 jigger Dry Gin.
1/3 jigger French Vermouth.
1/3 jigger Italian Vermouth.
1 Slice Orange.

Shake well; strain into Cocktail glass and serve.

BURNT BRANDY

Place two lumps of Cut Loaf Sugar in a small, shallow dish or
saucer and pour over the Sugar 1 1/2 jiggers of Cognac Brandy.
Ignite the Sugar and Brandy and let them burn for about
two minutes. Then cover the dish or saucer with a plate,
and when the fire is extinguished pour the liquid
into a small Bar glass and serve.

BUSTER BROWN COCKTAIL

Fill large Bar glass 2/3 full Shaved Ice.

1 teaspoonful Gum Syrup.

2 dashes Lemon Juice.

2 dashes Orange Bitters.

1 jigger Whiskey.

Stir; strain into Cocktail glass and serve.

BUTTERED RUM

In a Tumbler drop 1 lump of Sugar and dissolve it in a little hot Water, and add:

1 1/4 jiggers Rum.

1 piece of Butter about the size of a Walnut.

Grate Nutmeg on top and serve.

CALIFORNIA SHERRY COBBLER

1 pony of Pineapple Syrup in large Bar glass.

2 jiggers California Sherry.

Fill glass with Shaved Ice; stir well; decorate with Fruit; dash a little Port Wine on top and serve with Straws.

CALIFORNIA WINE COBBLER

Fill tall, thin glass nearly full Shaved Ice.

1 heaping teaspoonful Bar Sugar.

Juice of 1 Orange.

2 1/2 jiggers California Wine.

Stir; ornament with Fruit and serve with Straws.

Americans have drunk refreshingly icy Cobblers since at least 1809, when one was mentioned in Washington Irving's *History of New York*. Here, an ad informs readers of a 1900 *Munsey's Magazine* they can purchase six bottles of ten year old wine for $2.95.

"ONLY ONE MARRIAGE I REGRET. I REMEMBER AFTER I GOT THAT MARRIAGE LICENSE I WENT ACROSS FROM THE LICENSE BUREAU TO A BAR FOR A DRINK. THE BARTENDER SAID, 'WHAT WILL YOU HAVE, SIR?' AND I SAID, 'A GLASS OF HEMLOCK.'"

ERNEST HEMINGWAY
(1899–1961)

CARLETON RICKEY - St. Louis Style

Use a large Mixing glass; fill with Lump Ice.

Juice 1 Lime.

Drop squeezed Lime in glass.

1 jigger Old Bourbon Whiskey.

Fill with Sweet Soda.

Stir well and serve.

CATAWBA COBBLER

Fill large Bar glass 1/2 full of Shaved Ice.

1 teaspoonful Bar Sugar dissolved in a little Water.

1 1/2 jiggers Catawba Wine.

1/4 slice of Orange.

Fill with Shaved Ice; stir well; decorate with Berries and serve with Straws.

CELERY SOUR

Fill large Bar glass full Shaved Ice.

1 teaspoonful Lemon Juice.

1 teaspoonful Pineapple Syrup.

1 teaspoonful Celery Bitters.

Stir; strain into Fancy Wineglass with Fruit and serve.

CENTURY CLUB PUNCH (for a party of 5)

Fill glass Pitcher 1/4 full Cracked Ice.

1/2 pint Jamaica Rum.

1/2 pint Santa Cruz Rum.

2 1/2 pints aerated Water.

2 1/2 tablespoonfuls Bar Sugar.

Stir well and serve in Punch glasses.

CHAMPAGNE

Serve off the Ice very cold. Ice should never be put in the Wine.

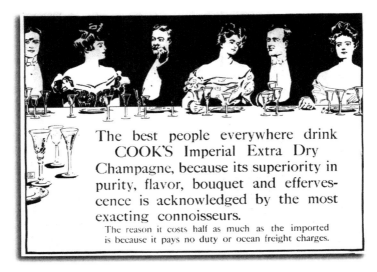

The best people everywhere drink COOK'S Imperial Extra Dry Champagne, because its superiority in purity, flavor, bouquet and effervescence is acknowledged by the most exacting connoisseurs.

The reason it costs half as much as the imported is because it pays no duty or ocean freight charges.

U.S. writer Bernard De Voto called the cocktail "... the supreme American gift to world culture." Here, a 1906 *Harper's Magazine* advertisement for Cook's Champagne states, "The best people everywhere drink Cook's ... ."

CHAMPAGNE COBBLER

I teaspoonful Bar Sugar in large Bar glass.

I slice Lemon Peel.

I slice Orange Peel.

Fill glass 1/2 full Shaved Ice and fill up with Champagne. Decorate with Fruit and serve with Straws.

CHAMPAGNE COCKTAIL

I lump Sugar in tall, thin glass.

I small piece Ice.

2 dashes Angostura Bitters.

I piece twisted Lemon Peel.

Fill up with Champagne.

Stir and serve.

CHAMPAGNE CUP

2-gallon mixture

For mixing use a large Punch bowl or other suitable vessel of glass
or porcelain lined.

4 Oranges, sliced.

4 Lemons, sliced.

1/2 Pineapple, sliced.

1/2 pint Chartreuse.

1/2 pint Abricontine.

1 pint Curacoa.

1 pint Cognac Brandy.

1 pint Tokay Wine.

Stir well and allow mixture to stand three hours. Strain into
another bowl and add:

3 quarts Champagne.

3 pints Apollinaris Water.

1 large piece of Ice.

Stir well; decorate with Fruit; float slices of Grape Fruit
on top and serve in Champagne glasses.

CHAMPAGNE FRAPPE

Place a bottle in a Champagne cooler and around it a freezing
mixture of fine Ice and Salt. Twirl the bottle until it is
about to freeze, when it will be ready to serve.

CHAMPAGNE JULEP

Fill medium size Shell glass 1/3 full Cracked Ice.

2 teaspoonfuls Bar Sugar.

2 sprigs bruised Mint.

Pour Champagne slowly into the glass,
stirring gently at the same time.

Dress with fruit; dash with Brandy and serve with Straws.

When 1899 turned to 1900, *Munsey's Magazine* readers were turning to Gold Seal Champagne. Here, a cherub toasts the new century and wishes readers a happy new year.

CHAMPAGNE PUNCH

for a party of 6

Into a glass Pitcher pour the Juice of 1 Lemon, and add:

1/4 lb. Bar Sugar.

1 jigger Strawberry Syrup.

1 quart bottle Champagne.

Stir with Ladle and drop in:

1 sliced Orange.

3 slices Pineapple.

Decorate with Fruit and serve in Champagne goblets.

CHAMPAGNE SOUR

Fill medium Bar glass 1/3 full Shaved Ice.
3 dashes Lemon Juice.
Fill up with Champagne.

Stir gently; dress with Fruit and Berries;
dash with Brandy and serve with Straws.

CHAMPAGNE VELVET

Fill Goblet 1/2 full ice-cold Champagne.
Fill up balance of Goblet with ice-cold Porter. Stir and serve.

CHOCOLATE PUNCH

Fill large Bar glass 2/3 full Shaved Ice.
1 teaspoonful Bar Sugar.
1/4 jigger Curacoa.
1 jigger Port Wine.
1 Egg.

Fill up with Milk; shake well; strain into Punch glass;
grate Nutmeg on top and serve.

CIDER EGGNOG

Into a large Bar glass break a fresh Egg.
1 teaspoonful Sugar.
4 lumps Cracked Ice.
Fill up with Sweet Cider.

Shake; strain into tall, thin glass and
serve with grated Nutmeg on top.

"Grandma says all these new dances and things are vulgar.
Do you see anything out of the way in them?" one lady asks another
in this June 19, 1913, *Life* magazine illustration.

CLARET AND ICE

4 lumps Ice in medium size Mineral Water glass.
Fill up with Claret and serve.

CLARET COBBLER

Dissolve one teaspoonful of Sugar with
little Water in large Bar glass.
1 quartered slice Orange.
2 jiggers Claret.

Fill up with Shaved Ice and serve with Straws.

CLARET CUP (2-gallon mixture)

For mixing use a large Punch bowl or other suitable vessel of glass or porcelain lined.

6 Oranges, sliced.

3 Lemons, sliced.

2 Pineapples.

2 jiggers Abricontine.

4 jiggers Curacoa.

4 quarts Claret.

3 pints Apollinaris.

Mix well with a Ladle and set aside for three hours before using. Then strain into another bowl, and when ready to use add 3 pints of some sparkling Wine, preferably Champagne. Stir gently once or twice, and then put in a block of clear Ice and decorate the top of it tastily with Fruits and let several slices of Grape Fruit float around in the bowl. Serve in Champagne glasses.

CLARET FLIP

Fill large Bar glass 1/2 full Shaved Ice.

2 heaping teaspoonfuls Bar Sugar dissolved in a little Water.

1 whole Egg broken in.

1 1/2 jiggers Claret Wine.

Shake thoroughly; strain into Punch glass;
sprinkle with Nutmeg on top and serve.

CLARET PUNCH

Fill large Bar glass 2/3 full Shaved Ice.

3 teaspoonfuls Bar Sugar.

4 dashes Lemon Juice.

2 slices Orange.

2 jiggers Claret.

Shake; strain into thin glass; dress with Fruit and serve with Straws.

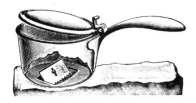
Many of Tom Bullock's recipes call for finely shaved ice.
Featured above, a labor-saving device from The Enterprise Mfg. Co.
"Simply draw the blade over a piece of ice, the pressure applied producing fine or coarse pieces, as desired," says this 1906 ad.

"CLARET IS THE LIQUOR FOR BOYS,
PORT FOR MEN; BUT HE WHO ASPIRES
TO BE A HERO MUST DRINK BRANDY."

SAMUEL JOHNSON
(1709 - 1784)

CLARET PUNCH

5-gallon mixture for a large reception or party of 100 people

For mixing use a large agate or porcelain-lined vessel.

4 lbs. Cut Loaf Sugar.

Juice of 25 Lemons.

2 quarts Brandy.

10 quarts Claret.

7 jiggers Chartreuse (green).

8 quarts Carbonated Water.

Stir well. Place a large block of Ice in a Punch bowl
and fill nearly full of the mixture, adding:

18 Oranges, cut in slices.

1 1/2 cans sliced Pineapples.

Serve from the bowl into Punch glasses with a Ladle, and renew
the contents of the bowl from the mixing vessel as needed.

CLOVER CLUB COCKTAIL

Fill large Bar glass 1/2 full Fine Ice.

1/2 pony Raspberry Syrup.

1/2 jigger Dry Gin.

1/2 jigger French Vermouth.

White of 1 Egg.

Shake well; strain into Cocktail glass and serve.

CLOVER LEAF COCKTAIL

Fill Mixing glass with Lump Ice.

1/2 pony Cusenier Grenadine.

The white of one Egg.

1 jigger Sir Robert Burnette's Old Tom Gin.

Shake well and strain into a Cocktail glass.

CLUB COCKTAIL

Fill large Bar glass 1/2 full Shaved Ice.

2 dashes Angostura Bitters.

2 dashes Pineapple Syrup.

1 jigger Brandy.

Stir; strain into Cocktail glass; dress with Berries;
dash with Champagne; twist a piece of Lemon Skin
over the drink and drop it on top. Serve.

CLUB HOUSE CLARET PUNCH

Fill large Bar glass 3/4 full Shaved Ice.

4 dashes Gum Syrup.

1 teaspoonful Lemon Juice.

1 teaspoonful Orange Juice.

2 jiggers Claret.

Shake; strain into tall, thin glass; fill up with Apollinaris
or seltzer; dress with Fruit and serve.

CLUB HOUSE PUNCH (for a party of 20)

For mixing use a large Punch bowl.

1/2 can Peaches.

1/2 can Pineapples.

3 Oranges, sliced.

3 Lemons, sliced.

3 quarts Sweet Catawba or Tokay.

1 pint Brandy.

1 1/2 jiggers Jamaica Rum.

1 jigger Green Chartreuse.

Set this mixture aside in ice box for 6 hours. Then place block
of Ice in another bowl of sufficient capacity and strain in
the mixture from the Mixing bowl. Dress the Ice with Fruit
and serve with a Ladle into Punch glasses.

White House brand tea and coffee advertisement
from the March 7, 1914 *New England Homestead*.

COFFEE COCKTAIL

Fill large Bar glass 2/3 full Shaved Ice.

1 fresh Egg.

1 teaspoonful Bar Sugar.

1 jigger Port Wine.

1 pony Brandy.

Shake; strain into medium thin glass; grate Nutmeg on top and serve.

COHASSET PUNCH

Fill large Bar glass 1/2 full Shaved Ice.
1 jigger New England Rum.
1 jigger Vermouth.
3 dashes Gum Syrup.
1 dash Orange Bitters.
1/2 juice of a Lemon.

Stir and serve with a Preserved Peach and its liquor.

COLD RUBY PUNCH

2 1/2-gallon mixture for 50 people

4 lbs. Cut Loaf Sugar.
2 quarts Port Wine.
2 quarts Batavia Arrack.
6 quarts green Tea.
Juice of 24 Lemons.
(See instructions for mixing and serving Punches in quantities.)

COLUMBIA SKIN

This drink is identical with Whiskey Skin.

COMPANION PUNCH

2 1/2-gallon mixture for a reception or party of 50 people

Into a large Punch bowl pour:
1 1/4 pints Lemon Juice.
2 pints Gum Syrup.
3/4 pint Orange Juice.
1 1/4 pints Brandy.
6 quarts equal parts Sweet and Dry Catawba.
2 quarts Carbonated Water.

When well stirred place large block of Ice in center of bowl;
dress the Ice with Fruit and serve with a Ladle into Punch glasses.

CONTINENTAL SOUR

Fill a large Bar glass 2/3 full Shaved Ice.
1 teaspoonful Bar Sugar dissolved in little Water.
Juice of 1/2 Lemon.
1 jigger of Whiskey, Brandy or Gin, as preferred.

Shake; strain into Sour glass; dash with Claret and serve.

COOPERSTOWN COCKTAIL

Use a large Bar glass.
Fill with Lump Ice.
One jigger of Sir Robert Burnette's Old Tom Gin.
1/2 pony of Italian Vermouth.
Six leaves of fresh Mint.
Shake ingredients well together.

Strain and serve in Cocktail glass.

CORDIAL LEMONADE

Add to a plain Lemonade 1/3 jigger of any Cordial
which the customer may prefer, and serve.

COUNTRY CLUB PUNCH

Take 1 1/2 lbs. of Cut Loaf Sugar and rub the lumps on the skins
of 4 Lemons and 2 Oranges until the Sugar becomes well saturated
with the oil from the skins. Then put the Sugar thus prepared
into a large porcelain-lined or agate Mixing vessel, and add:
12 Oranges, sliced.
1 Pineapple, sliced.
1 box Strawberries.
2 bottles (quarts) Apollinaris Water.

COUNTRY CLUB PUNCH (continued)

Stir thoroughly with oak paddle or large silver ladle, and add:

1 jigger Benedictine.
1 jigger Red Curacoa.
1 jigger Maraschino.
1/2 jigger Jamaica Rum.
1 quart Brandy.
4 quarts Tokay or Sweet Catawba Wine.
2 quarts Madeira Wine.
4 quarts Chateau Margaux.

Mix well with oak paddle or ladle and strain into another bowl
in which has been placed a block of clear ice. Then pour in
6 quarts Champagne. Decorate the Ice with Fruits, Berries, etc.
Serve in Punch cups or glasses, dressing each glass with
Fruit and Berries from the bowl.

COUNTRY COCKTAIL

Fill large Bar glass 2/3 full Shaved Ice.
1 teaspoonful Bar Sugar.
1 pony Brandy.
1 jigger Port Wine.
1 Egg.

Shake well; strain into thin glass; grate Nutmeg on top and serve.

COUPEREE

Fill large Bar glass 1/3 full Ice Cream.
3/4 jigger Brandy.
1 pony Red Curacoa.
Mix thoroughly with a spoon.

Fill up with Plain Soda; grate Nutmeg on top and serve.

CREME DE MENTHE

Fill a Sherry glass with Shaved Ice.
1 pony Creme de Menthe.
Cut Straw in two pieces and serve.

CRIMEAN CUP A LA MARMORA

for a party of 10

Into a small Punch bowl pour:
1 pint Orgeat Syrup.
2 jiggers Jamaica Rum.
2 jiggers Maraschino.
2 1/2 jiggers Brandy.
2 tablespoonfuls Bar Sugar.
1 quart Champagne.
1 quart Plain Soda.

Stir well; pack the bowl in Fine Ice,
and when cold serve in fancy Stem glasses.

CURACOA

Into a bottle which will hold a full quart, or a little over,
drop 6 ounces of Orange Peel sliced very thin,
and add 1 pint of Whiskey. Cork the bottle securely and let it
stand two weeks, shaking the bottle frequently during that time.
Next strain the mixture, add the Syrup, pour the strained
mixture back into the cleaned bottle and let it stand 3 days,
shaking well now and then during the first day.
Next, pour a teacupful of the mixture into a mortar and
beat up with it 1 drachm Powdered Alum, 1 drachm Carbonate
of Potash. Put this mixture back into the bottle and let it stand
for 10 days, at the expiration of which time the Curacoa
will be clear and ready for use.

Maraschino liqueur is one of the primary ingredients in
Crimean Cup a la Marmora, a tasty punch for small parties.
The name of this drink may have been inspired by the Crimean war
of 1853-1856 or simply attributed to Crimea because Maraschino
is made from the fermented juice of the marasca, a sour cherry grown
in that area and located directly across from the in-land sea of Marmora.

Featured above, Maraschino ad from 1905.

CURACOA PUNCH

Fill large Bar glass 3/4 full Shaved Ice.
2 teaspoonfuls Bar Sugar.
4 dashes Lemon Juice.
1 pony Red Curacoa.
1 jigger Brandy.
1/2 pony Jamaica Rum.

Stir; decorate with Fruit and Serve with Straws.

Delicious cherry, raspberry, or other small fruit Shrubs can be made weeks ahead and served by the glass. The Shrub allegedly originated in merry old England, but its name came from the Arabic word for drink, "surb." For the kiddies or abstainers, nonalcoholic Shrubs can be mixed from fruit juice, vinegar, and sugar and served immediately.

Illustration from New England Homestead.

CURRANT SHRUB

For mixing use a porcelain-lined or agate vessel, and put in:

1 1/2 lbs. Cut Loaf Sugar.
1 quart Currant Juice.

Place vessel on the fire and let it boil slowly for 10 minutes, and skim well while boiling. Then remove vessel from fire and add 1/2 gill of Brandy to every pint of Shrub. Bottle and cork securely. This drink is served by simply pouring a little of the Syrup into Ice Water, as any drink from Fruit Syrup is prepared. The basis preparation for all Shrubs or Small Fruits, such as Cherries, Raspberries, etc., is prepared in the same way as directed for Currant Shrub, varying the quantity of Sugar used to suit the kind of Fruit.

DELUSION

Use a large Mixing glass; fill with Shaved Ice.

1/2 Lime Juice.

2/3 white Creme de Menthe.

1/3 Apricot Brandy.

Shake well; strain into thin Stem glass and serve.

DERONDA COCKTAIL

Fill large Bar glass with Shaved Ice.

1 1/2 jiggers Calisaya.

1 1/2 jiggers Plymouth Gin.

Shake; strain into Cocktail glass and serve.

DIARRHEA DRAUGHT

Into a Whiskey glass pour:

1/2 jigger Blackberry Brandy.

1/2 pony Peach Brandy.

2 dashes Jamaica Ginger.

Grate Nutmeg on top and serve.

DIXIE COCKTAIL

Add to a plain Whiskey Cocktail:

1 dash Curacoa.

6 drops Creme de Menthe.

DORAY PUNCH

Fill large Bar glass 2/3 full Shaved Ice.

2 teaspoonfuls Lemon Juice.

4 dashes Pineapple Syrup.

4 dashes Gum Syrup.

1/4 jigger Jamaica Rum.

1/4 jigger green Chartreuse.

1/2 jigger Tokay Wine.

1/2 jigger Brandy.

1 white of an Egg.

Shake hard; strain into thin Bar glass; dress with Fruit;
dash with Seltzer; grate Nutmeg on top and serve.

DORAY SOUR

Fill large Bar glass 2/3 full Shaved Ice.

3 dashes Gum Syrup.

4 dashes Lemon Juice.

1 dash Lime Juice.

1 teaspoonful Abricontine or green Chartreuse.

1/2 jigger Tokay or Sweet Catawba Wine.

1/2 jigger Brandy.

Stir well and strain into a fancy Sour glass;
dress with Fruits, dash with Apollinaris or Seltzer;
top off with a little Claret and serve.

DREAM

Fill large Bar glass 2/3 full Shaved Ice.

1 teaspoonful Bar Sugar.

3 dashes Lemon Juice.

1 white of an Egg.

1 Wineglass Milk and Cream.

1 jigger Tom Gin.

Shake thoroughly; strain into tall, thin glass;
cover the top lightly with Creme de Menthe and serve.

Esportazione del

vero

Vino Vermouth di Torino

tipico, preparato con

VINO MOSCATO DI CANELLI

e di

Vini genuini, tipici del Piemonte

dell'antica Casa

(fondata nel 1850)

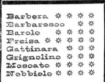

FRATELLI GANCIA E C.

di CANELLI.

A double dose of Vermouth gave the Duplex Cocktail its name.
During Tom Bullock's bartending days, sweet vermouth came from
Italy and dry Vermouth came from France.

Here, an Italian Vermouth ad from 1905.

DUPLEX COCKTAIL

Fill large Bar glass with Shaved Ice.

1/3 jigger Old Tom Gin.

1 pony Italian Vermouth.

1 pony French Vermouth.

3 dashes Acid Phosphate.

4 dashes Orange Bitters.

Shake; strain into Cocktail glass and serve.

DURKEE COCKTAIL

Fill large Bar glass 2/3 full Shaved Ice.

1 tablespoonful Bar Sugar.

4 dashes Lemon Juice.

3 dashes Curacoa.

1 jigger Jamaica Rum.

Shake well; strain into tall, thin glass;
fill up with Plain Soda; stir gently and serve.

EAGLE PUNCH

Into a Hot Water glass drop:

1 lump Cut Loaf Sugar and dissolve in little Hot Water,
crushing with muddler.

1/2 jigger Bourbon Whiskey.

1/2 jigger Rye Whiskey.

Fill up with boiling Water; twist a piece of Lemon Peel
and grate Nutmeg on top and serve.

EAST INDIA COCKTAIL

Fill large Bar glass 3/4 full Shaved Ice.

3 dashes Maraschino.

3 dashes Red Curacoa.

3 dashes Angostura Bitters.

1 jigger Brandy.

Stir well; strain into Cocktail glass and serve with
a piece of twisted Lemon Peel on top.

EGG MILK PUNCH

Fill large Bar glass 1/2 full Shaved Ice.

2 teaspoonfuls Bar Sugar.

1 Egg

1 pony Santa Cruz Rum.

1 jigger Brandy.

Fill up with Milk; shake thoroughly until the mixture creams; strain into tall thin glass; grate Nutmeg on top and serve.

EGGNOG

Fill large Bar glass 1/2 full Shaved Ice.

1 Egg.

1 teaspoonful Bar Sugar.

3/4 jigger Brandy.

1/2 jigger Jamaica Rum.

Fill up with Milk; shake thoroughly; strain into tall, thin glass and serve with little Nutmeg grated on top.

EGGNOG (bowl of 3 gallons)

Beat the yolks of 20 Eggs until thin and stir in 2 1/2 lbs. Bar Sugar until Sugar is thoroughly dissolved. Into this mixture pour:

1 1/2 pints Jamaica Rum.

2 quarts old Brandy.

Mix the ingredients well by stirring. Then pour in the milk slowly, stirring all the while to prevent curdling. Pour carefully over the top of the mixture the whites of the Eggs, which have been beaten to a stiff froth. Fill Punch glasses from the bowl with ladle and sprinkle a little Nutmeg over each glassful.

EGG SOUR

Into small Bar glass drop:

3 lumps Ice.

1 tablespoonful Bar Sugar.

1 Egg.

Juice of 1 Lemon.

Shake well; grate Nutmeg on top and serve with Straw.

EL DORADO PUNCH

Fill large Bar glass nearly full Shaved Ice.

1 tablespoonful Bar Sugar.

1/4 jigger Whiskey.

1/4 jigger Jamaica Rum.

1/2 jigger Brandy.

1 slice Lemon.

Shake; dress with Fruit and serve with Straws.

ENGLISH BISHOP PUNCH

Roast an Orange before a fire or in a hot oven. When brown
cut it in quarters and drop the pieces, with a few Cloves,
into a small porcelain-lined or agate vessel, and pour in 1 quart
of hot Port Wine. Add 6 lumps Cut Loaf Sugar and
let the mixture simmer over the fire for 30 minutes.
Serve in Stem glasses with Nutmeg grated on top.

FANCY WHISKEY SMASH

Fill large Bar glass 1/2 full Shaved Ice.

2 teaspoonfuls Bar Sugar.

3 sprigs Mint pressed with muddler in 1 jigger aerated Water.

1 jigger Whiskey.

Stir well; strain into Sour glass; dress with Fruit and serve.

A RECEIPT FOR KISSES.

TO ONE PIECE OF DARK PIAZZA AND A LITTLE MOONLIGHT—TAKE FOR GRANTED TWO PEOPLE. PRESS IN TWO STRONG ONES A SMALL,
SOFT HAND. SIFT LIGHTLY TWO OUNCES OF ATTRACTION, ONE OF ROMANCE ; ADD A LARGE MEASURE OF FOLLY ; STIR IN A FLOATING
RUFFLE AND ONE OR TWO WHISPERS.   DISSOLVE HALF A DOZEN GLANCES IN A WELL OF SILENCE ; DUST IN A SMALL QUANTITY OF
HESITATION, ONE OUNCE OF RESISTANCE, TWO OF YIELDING ; PLACE THE KISSES ON A FLUSHED CHEEK OR TWO LIPS, FLAVOR WITH A
SLIGHT SCREAM, AND SET ASIDE TO COOL.   THIS WILL SUCCEED IN ANY CLIMATE, IF DIRECTIONS ARE CAREFULLY FOLLOWED.

The caption on this 1900 Charles Dana Gibson print says:

A Receipt [Recipe] For Kisses:
To one piece of dark piazza and a little moonlight — take for granted two people.
Press in two strong ones a small, soft hand. Sift lightly two ounces of attraction,
one of romance; add a large measure of folly; stir in a floating ruffle and one or two whispers.
Dissolve half a dozen glances in a well of silence; dust in a small quantity of hesitation,
one ounce of resistance, two of yielding; place the kisses on a flushed cheek or two lips;
flavor with a slight scream, and set aside to cool.
This will succeed in any climate, if directions are carefully followed.

FANNIE WARD

Use a large Mixing glass with Lump Ice.
White of an Egg.
Juice 1/2 Lime.
2 dashes imported Grenadine.
1 jigger Bacardi Rum.

Shake and strain into Cocktail glass.

FEDORA

Fill large Bar glass 3/4 full Shaved Ice.
2 teaspoonfuls Bar Sugar dissolved in little Water.
1 pony Curacoa.
1 pony Brandy.
1/2 pony Jamaica Rum.
1/2 pony Whiskey.

Shake well; dress with Fruit and serve with Straws.

FISH CLUB PUNCH

for a party of 8

Into a Punch bowl pour:
2 1/2 jiggers Lemon Juice.
4 jiggers Peach Brandy.
2 jiggers Cognac Brandy.
2 jiggers Jamaica Rum.
3 pints Ice Water.
Stir well; ladle into Punch glass and serve.

FOG HORN - Country Club Style

Use a large Mixing glass; fill with Lump Ice.
1/2 Lime Juice.
1/2 Lemon Juice.
1 teaspoonful Bar Sugar.
1 jigger Burnette's Old Tom Gin.

Stir well; strain into tall, thin glass and fill with imported Ginger Ale.

This leather postcard from 1906 disparages the temperance-minded women who marched for prohibition from 1873 to 1920. The lady in it probably didn't inspire Mr. Bullock's "FREE LOVE COCKTAIL." Rather, the cocktail's name came from the Free Love movement that spread across Europe in the 1860s and reached its U.S. height in the 1890s.

FREE LOVE COCKTAIL - Club Style

Lump Ice.
Use Shaker.
1/2 of the white of 1 Egg.
3 dashes Anisette.
1 jigger Old Tom Gin.
1 pony fresh Cream.

Shake well, serve in Cocktail glass.

FRENCH POUSSE CAFE

Fill a Pousse Cafe glass 1/2 full of Maraschino and add:
Raspberry Syrup, Vanilla, Curacoa, Chartreuse and
Brandy in equal proportions until the glass is filled.
Then proceed as for ABRICONTINE POUSSE CAFE.

GARDEN PUNCH

2 1/2 –gallon mixture for a party of 50

Place a good size block of Ice in a large Punch bowl.
4 jiggers Lemon Juice.
1 1/2 lbs. Bar Sugar.
2 jiggers Orange Juice.
1 1/2 jiggers green Chartreuse.
1 quart Brandy.
6 quarts Tokay or Sweet Catawba Wine.
2 quarts Claret Wine.

Stir well; ladle into Stem glasses,
and decorate each glass with Fruit before serving.

GIBSON COCKTAIL

Use a large Mixing glass with Lump Ice.
1 jigger Gordon Gin.
1 pony French Vermouth.

Stir; strain and serve in Cocktail glass.

GILLETTE COCKTAIL - Chicago Style

Use a large Mixing glass; fill with Lump Ice.
Juice 1/2 Lime.
1 1/2 jiggers Burnette's Old Tom Gin.
1/2 teaspoonful Bar Sugar.

Stir well and strain into Cocktail glass.

The "United"
Concentrated
Extracts

Supply the Missing Link That You Have Been Looking for

Created to appeal to the Taste with a Distinct and inimitable Non-Alcoholic Flavor and made Refreshing to Satisfy All Sufferers from Imitations, Poor Quality, Cheap Ingredients and Unsanitary Substitutes. Also to Meet the Demand of People who want only the Best Possible.

The "United" Concentrated Extracts are Guaranteed to be Above the Sanitary Requirements, to be Pure and made only from Healthy Ingredients, Vegetables, Cereals and Fruit, that will in no way Harm, but bring Happy Smiles and Old Memories of By-Gone Days.

$1.00 TRIAL SIZE SENT BY REQUEST

There's Something About Them You'll Like

ONE PINT—$16.00

SIX PINTS—$80.00

ONE GALLON—$100.00

During Prohibition, gin was often distilled in the bathtub and aged during the time it took the maker to carry it from the tub to the party. Some companies, like United Beverage, survived during Prohibition by selling "flavors" of Grain (pictured above), Vermouth, and Juniper (for making gin).

Advertisement from United Beverage catalog, 1921.

GIN AND CALAMUS

Put 1/2 oz. of Calamus Root, which has been steeped,
into a quart bottle of Gin.

Serve as you would a Straight Drink.

GIN DAISY

Juice of 1/2 of a Lime.
1 pony Cusenier Grenadine.
1 jigger Sir Robert Burnette's Old Tom Gin.
Serve in a Mug with Lump Ice; fill with Seltzer.

Stir well and decorate with the skin of the Lime
and fresh Mint and serve with Straws.

GIN SOUR - Country Club Style

Use a large Mixing glass.
Fill with Lump Ice.
1/2 Lime Juice.
1/2 Orange Juice.
2 dashes Pineapple Juice.
1/2 pony Rock Candy Syrup.
1 jigger Burnette's Old Tom Gin.

Shake well; strain into Cocktail glass and serve.

GIN SQUASH - Country Club Style

Use a large glass Stein; fill with Lump Ice.
1 pony Lemon Juice.
1 jigger Orange Juice.
1 pony Pineapple Juice.
1 pony Rock Candy Syrup.
1 jigger Burnette's Old Tom Gin.

Fill with Seltzer: stir well and serve.

GOLFER'S DELIGHT –
HOME OF BEVO – 18TH HOLE

Use a large glass Pitcher; fill with Lump Ice.
2 bottles Bevo.
2 bottles Sweet Soda.

Stir well and serve in a Beer glass.
Fifty-fifty.

G.O.P.

Use a large Mixing glass with Lump of Ice.
2 jiggers of Orange Juice.
2 jiggers of Grape Fruit Juice.
Fill with Seltzer Water.

Stir; ornament with Fruit and serve with Straws.

HORSE THIEF COCKTAIL

Fill a large Mixing glass with Lump Ice.
2 dashes green Absinthe.
1/2 pony Italian Vermouth.
1 jigger Sir Robert Burnette's Old Tom Gin.

Stir well and serve in a Cocktail glass.

IRISH ROSE - Country Club Style

Use a tall, thin glass; fill with Cracked Ice.
1 pony imported Grenadine.
1 jigger Old Bushmill Whiskey.
Fill with Seltzer.

Stir well and serve.

BEVO—A Real Thirst Quencher at the 19th Hole

Tom Bullock probably developed his GOLFER'S DELIGHT recipe to honor patron August A. Busch, Sr. Mr. Busch began distributing Bevo, the first non-alcoholic beer, about the same time Tom Bullock completed his book *The Ideal Bartender*. Bevo was one of several non-alcoholic products that helped keep Anheuser-Busch solvent and its employees employed during prohibition.

Watercolor courtesy of Anheuser-Busch, Inc.

JERSEY LIGHTNING COCKTAIL

Use large Mixing glass; fill with Lump Ice.

1 jigger Apple Jack Brandy.

1 pony Italian Vermouth.

Stir well; strain and serve in Cocktail glass.

KNABENSCHUE - Country Club Style

Use a small stone Mug; Lump Ice.

1 lump Sugar.

2 dashes Angostura Bitters.

Fill with Champagne.

Stir well; dress with fresh Mint and serve.

LADIES' DELIGHT -
Thursday Luncheon Punch

1 quart of Orange Pekoe Tea (cold).
1 quart of Old Country Club Brandy.
1 pint of Lemon Juice.
1 pint of Orange Juice.
1/2 pint of Pineapple Juice.
2 quarts Berncastler Berg.
1 pint of Bar Sugar.

Use a large Punch bowl with one Lump of Ice.
Pour in mixture; add one quart of Cook's Imperial Champagne.
Stir well; decorate with fresh Mint, Fruit in season, and serve.

LEAPING FROG

1 jigger Hungarian Apricot Brandy.
Juice of 1/2 Lime.
Fill glass with Lump Ice.

Shake well and strain into Stem glass.

LEMONADE APOLLINARIS

or carbonated water

Fill large Mixing glass 2/3 full fine Ice.
1 tablespoonful Bar Sugar.
Juice of 1 Lemon.

Fill up with Apollinaris or suitable Carbonated Water.
Stir; strain into Lemonade glass; dress with Fruit and serve.

LONE TREE COCKTAIL

Use a large Mixing glass; fill with Lump Ice.
1 jigger Burnette's Old Tom Gin.
1/3 Italian Vermouth.
1/3 French Vermouth.

Shake well; serve in Cocktail glass.

L. P. W.

Use a large Mixing glass.
Fill with Lump Ice.
1 jigger of Sir Robert Burnette's Old Tom Gin.
1/2 pony of Italian Vermouth.
1/2 pony of French Vermouth.

Stir well and strain into a Cocktail glass.
Add a Pickeled Onion and serve.

MINT JULEP - Kentucky Style

Use a large Silver Mug.
Dissolve one lump of Sugar in one-half pony of Water.
Fill mug with Fine Ice.
Two jiggers of Old Bourbon Whiskey.

Stir well; add one boquet of Mint and serve.
Be careful and not bruise the Mint.

OJEN COCKTAIL

Use an old-fashion Toddy glass.
1 lump Ice.
Juice of 1/2 of a Lime.
1 dash Angostura Bitters.
2 dashes of Seltzer Water.

Stir well and serve.

Tom Bullock emphasizes the importance of choosing quality water throughout his 1917 cocktail book, *The Ideal Bartender*.

Here, an advertisement for
White Rock Mineral Water from 1921.

OLD FASHION COCKTAIL

Use a Toddy glass.
1 lump of Ice.
2 dashes of Angostura Bitters.
1 lump of Sugar and dissolve in Water.
1 1/2 jiggers of Bourbon Whiskey.

Twist piece of Lemon Skin over the drink and drop it in.
Stir well and serve.

ONION COCKTAIL

1 jigger of Burnette's Tom Gin.
1/2 of Italian Vermouth and no Bitters used.
Large Bar glass with Cracked Ice and stir well.

Strain and serve with an Onion.

Cocktails, wine, and beer were served in luxury train cars, the preferred mode of transportation for wealthy travelers, as early as the 1870s.

Here, a 19th Century beverage menu courtesy of the B&O Railroad Museum.

OVERALL JULEP - St. Louis Style

Use a large Mixing glass; fill with Lump Ice.
2/3 Wineglass Rye Whiskey.
2/3 Wineglass Gordon Gin.
1/2 Wineglass Imported Grenadine.
Juice 1/2 Lemon.
Juice 1/2 Lime.

Shake well; pour into tall, thin glass;
add one bottle Imported Club Soda and serve.

PEQUOT SEMER

Use a tall, thin Bar glass.
Juice of a Lime.
Three sprigs of fresh Mint.
1 dash Cusinier Grenadine.
1/2 pony Pineapple Juice.
1/2 pony Orange Juice.
1 jigger of Sir Robert Burnette's Old Tom Gin.

Crush ingredients together; fill with Lump Ice; add Seltzer.
Stir well and serve.

PINEAPPLE JULEP

for a party of 6 – Use a small punch bowl
1 quart of Sparkling Moselle.
1 jigger Cusenier Grenadine.
1 jigger Maraschino.
1 jigger Sir Robert Burnette's Old Tom Gin.
1 jigger Lemon Juice.
1 jigger Orange Bitters.
1 jigger Angostura Bitters.
4 Oranges, sliced.
2 Lemons, sliced.
1 ripe Pineapple, sliced and quartered.
4 tablespoonfuls Sugar.
1 bottle Apollinaris Water.

Place large square of Ice in bowl; dress with the Fruits and
serve Julep in fancy Stem glass.

POLO PLAYERS' DELIGHT - Horse's Neck

Use a tall, thin glass.
1 lump Ice.
1 jigger Sir Robert Burnette's Old Tom Gin.
1 Cantrell & Cochran's Ginger Ale.

Stir well and serve.

POUSSE CAFE - St. Louis

Pour in Pousse Cafe glass as follows:
1/6 glass Raspberry Syrup.
1/6 glass Maraschino.
1/6 glass Green Vanilla.
1/6 glass Curacao.
1/6 glass Yellow Chartreuse.
1/6 glass Brandy.

In preparing the above use a small Wineglass
with spoon for pouring in each Cordial separately.
Be careful they do not mix together.

PUNCH A LA ROMAINE

for a party of 16
1 bottle Champagne.
1 bottle Rum.
2 tablespoons Dr. Siegert's genuine Angostura Bitters.
10 Lemons.
3 sweet Oranges.
2 pounds Powdered Sugar.
10 fresh Eggs.

Dissolve the Sugar in the Juice of the Lemons and Oranges
adding the Rind of 1 Orange. Strain through a Sieve into a bowl
and add by degrees the whites of the Eggs beaten to a froth.
Place the bowl on Ice till cold, then stir in the Rum and Wine
until thoroughly mixed. Serve in fancy Stem glasses.

RAMOS GIN FIZZ - Country Club Style

1 lump Ice.
1 dash Lemon Juice.
1 dash Orange Water.
White of Egg.
1 jigger Burnette's Old Tom Gin.
1 teaspoonful Powdered Sugar.
1 pony Milk.
1 dash Seltzer Water.

Shake well; strain into Highball glass and serve.

REMSEN COOLER

Use a medium size Fizz glass.
Peel a Lemon as you would an Apple.
Place the Rind or Peeling into the Fizz glass.
2 or 3 lumps of Crystal Ice.
1 Wineglass of Remsen Scotch Whiskey.

Fill up the balance with Club Soda;
stir up slowly with a spoon and serve.

In this country it is often the case that people call
a Remsen Cooler where they want Old Tom Gin or
Sloe Gin instead of Scotch Whiskey. It is therefore the
bartender's duty to mix as desired.

SEE THE LITTLE OLD-WORLD VILLAGE
WHERE HER AGED PARENTS LIVE,
DRINKING THE CHAMPAGNE SHE SENDS THEM;
BUT THEY NEVER CAN FORGIVE.

SONG FROM WORLD WAR I (1914-1918)

The Shandy Gaff, British slang for water (gatter) from a
public house (shandy), may have been developed in the 1700s,
but it's a delicious alternative for any calorie-or alcohol-conscious
person. In this advertisement, Schlitz warns us that beer exposed to
light for 5 minutes becomes undrinkable.

SAMTON COCKTAIL

Use a large Mixing glass with Cracked Ice.
1 jigger Orange Juice.
1 jigger imported Ginger Ale.
Fifty-Fifty.

Shake well; strain into Cocktail glass and serve.

SEPTEMBER MORN COCKTAIL - Country Club Style

Use a large Mixing glass; fill with Lump Ice.
1/2 Lime Juice.
1 jigger Burnette's Old Tom Gin.
2 dashes Imported Grenadine.

Shake well; strain into Cocktail glass and serve.

SHANDY GAFF

Use a large Bar glass.
Fill half the glass with Porter and half with Ginger Ale.
It is also made with half Ale and half Ginger Ale.

SHERRY AND BITTERS

Put 2 dashes Dr. Siegert's genuine Angostura Bitters
in a Sherry glass and roll the glass 'till the Bitters
entirely cover the inside surface.

Fill the glass with Sherry and serve.

STINGER - Country Club Style

Use a large Mixing glass; fill with Lump Ice.
1 jigger Old Brandy.
1 pony white Creme de Menthe.

Shake well; strain into Cocktail glass and serve.

HUNTER
BALTIMORE RYE
AN IDEAL PRODUCT OF THE STILL

Sold at all first-class cafes and by jobbers.
WM. LANAHAN & SON, Baltimore, Md.

Rye has been popular in the United States since the 1700s,
when immigrants from Germany and Northern Ireland settled,
bringing favorite recipes with them.

Advertisement from Leslie's Weekly, September 25, 1902.

STONE SOUR

Use a tall, thin glass; fill with fine Ice.

1/2 pony Lemon Juice.

1/2 pony Orange Juice.

2 dashes Rock Candy Syrup.

1 jigger Old Tom Gin.

Leave in Ice; stir well and serve.

TOKAY PUNCH

Out of 6 pounds of Tokay Grapes, select one pound to be put
into the Punch last. Now make a boiling Syrup of three pounds
of Sugar and one quart of boiling Water and pour this over
the remaining five pounds of Grapes. When partly cold rub it
through a sieve, leaving skins and seeds behind. Then add
the Juice of two Oranges and two Lemons and one quart of
St. Julien Claret, 1 jigger of Angostura Bitters.
Then strain and freeze. Before serving add 1 pint of good
Brandy and an Italian Meringue Paste of six Egg whites,
colored a nice red and drop in the remaining Grapes.

TOM AND JERRY

Make a batter by separating the yolks from whites of
a given number of Eggs; beating the whites to a stiff froth
and stirring the yolks until very thin. Then mix together in
a Tom and Jerry bowl, stirring in Bar Sugar slowly until
the batter is stiff and serve as follows:

Fill Tom and Jerry Mug 1/4 full of Batter.
1/2 jigger Rum.
1/2 jigger Brandy.

Stir well with Bar spoon; fill up with Hot Water; stir more;
grate Nutmeg on top and serve.

TOM TOM

Use a large Brandy Roller glass.
Fill Roller half full of Fine Ice.
Add 1 pony of Old Brandy.
1 jigger of green Creme de Menthe and serve.

TWILIGHT COCKTAIL

Use a large Mixing glass with Lump Ice.
1 jigger Bourbon.
1/2 pony Italian Vermouth.
Juice of whole Lime.

Shake well; strain into a Champagne glass;
fill with Seltzer and serve.

....

"ONCE DURING PROHIBITION I WAS FORCED TO LIVE FOR DAYS ON NOTHING BUT FOOD AND WATER."

W. C. FIELDS (1880-1946)

....

"THE COCKTAIL, TO MULTITUDES
OF FOREIGNERS, SEEMS TO BE
THE GREATEST SYMBOL OF THE
AMERICAN WAY OF LIFE."

H. L. MENCKEN
(1880-1956)

WHISKEY IRISH HOT

Substitute Irish for Scotch Whiskey and
proceed as for Hot Scotch Whiskey.

WHISKEY PUNCH - St. Louis Style

Use a large Mixing glass; fill with Lump Ice.
One jigger Bourbon Whiskey.
1/2 pony Italian Vermouth.
1/2 pony Pineapple Syrup.
1/2 pony Lemon Juice.

Shake well; strain into Stem glass and serve.

WHISKEY SCOTCH HOT

1 lump Sugar dissolved in Hot Whiskey glass.
1 jigger Scotch Whiskey.
Fill up with Hot Water.
1 slice Lemon Peel.

Stir and serve with Nutmeg sprinkled on top.

Behind Tom Bullock's Bar

Abricontine: The brand name of a brandy-based apricot liqueur made in France.

Absinthe: Whether you call it "The Green Menace," "The Green Goddess," "The Green Muse," or "The Green Fairy," you probably can't legally call for this bitter licorice-tasting liqueur at your local bar or club unless you live in Spain, Turkey, or, very recently, Great Britain.

Although Tom Bullock had been able to legally serve Absinthe for most of his working years, he couldn't legally serve it in 1917 at the time he wrote his opus, *The Ideal Bartender*. Still, in his book he included seven recipes that specify Absinthe as an ingredient and we've included them here for, well, historical purposes.

And why not? Dr. Pierre Ordinaire developed Absinthe as a tonic in 1792. Hippocrates, the greatest physician of western civilization, recommended something similar (wormwood in wine) as a remedy for several diseases.

By the 1850s, Absinthe was a favorite drink of the upper classes and by the 1870s everyone was drinking it. In fact, by Tom's time, the turn of the 19th century, Absinthe symbolized the wild beauty and artistic advances of chic and sophisticated belle époque Paris.

Problem was, Absinthe had too many people seeing more than green. It reportedly has hallucinogenic properties derived from one of its ingredients, wormwood.

By 1905, critics were saying it caused mutilations, violent murders, and even named a disease after it (absinthism, characterized by addiction, hallucinations, excitability, tremors, convulsions, and paralysis).

Absinthe has been illegal in the U.S. since 1912, Switzerland since 1908, and France since 1915. We can't recommend you order it off the internet from one of the countries where it is legal, so we offer some readily available licorice-flavored wormwood-free alternatives for your consideration:

- Anisados (Spain)
- Anisette (France)
- Herbsaint (France)
- Ouzo (Greece)
- Pastis (France)
- Pernod (France)
- Sambuca (Italy)

When you experiment with these already-sweetened Absinthe substitutes, keep in mind that the real thing is bitter and turns milky-white when water is added. You might want to omit the sugar from Mr. Bullock's recipes to accommodate your taste.

Absinthe Glass: Tom Bullock, like most bartenders of his day, probably used a special "Absinthe" glass with a hole leading to a glass bowl at the bottom. The bowl usually held shaved ice and water.

Absinthe Spoon: Absinthe is bitter, so the liqueur was usually sweetened by the drink by pouring it over sugar cubes placed in a slotted spoon.

Absinthe glass and spoon.
Illustration courtesy Steve Quinn

Admiral Schley: At the turn of the century, bartenders sometimes named the drinks they developed in honor of favorite patrons, to commemorate a special event, or after the establishment they served in. Mr. Bullock may have developed the Admiral Schley and named it after American naval commander Winfield Scott Schley (1839-1911) who served in the Spanish-American War (1898) and rescued Arctic explorer Adolphus W. Greeley.

Apple Jack: Mr. Bullock used various spellings when he referred to a U.S. brandy made from apples. Applejack is still produced on the East Coast, but is not as readily available as Calvados, a similar blend of apple and pear brandy from Normandy.

Arf & Arf: The English called it "Half & Half" when they mixed equal parts Guinness stout and Irish ale, but the Irish said it in their best rolling brogue and it sounded more like "Arf & Arf." A good Irishman would never dream of mixing an English stout and Irish ale in the same glass.

Apollinaris: Tom Bullock often requested Apollinaris sparkling mineral water by name in his recipes. "The Queen of Table Waters" is still being imported from Germany.

Arak: An aromatic rice-based rum common in Asia and the Middle East and popular in 17th century England. Arak is flavored with palms, dates, grains, grapes and has a licorice flavor. It's often the basis of grogs or punches, although it may be enjoyed straight. Some say it's not good for your health because of an alleged strong fuel oil/acid combination. See also: Arrak and Batavia-Arak.

Armagnac: This cousin of Cognac is slightly older and receives slightly more aging. Prolific French writer with African roots, Alexander Dumas (1802-1870), honors it in *The Three Musketeers* and *Le Grand Dictionnaire de Cuisine.*

Arrack: Tom Bullock sometimes uses this spelling for what is now more commonly known as Arak, or Raki.

Auditorium Cooler: Before air-conditioning, heat stroke and other dangerous medical conditions often occurred in auditoriums when people gathered together for student graduations and other events. Tom's Auditorium Cooler, a heat-taming thirst-quencher, was non-alcoholic so it could be enjoyed by the ladies and the kiddies.

Bar Glass: A mixing glass or stirring glass. Most bartenders use a stainless steel container topped with a glass mixing glass. This combo stops liquors from spilling and is often called a Boston shaker.

Barspoon: A spoon with a long handle, often used for mixing drinks in a tall bar glass.

Bar Sugar: At the turn of the century, sugar was often pressed into a block or "bar" and then wrapped in paper when sold.

Batavia Arak: Batavia is the old Dutch colonial name for Jakarta, Indonesia, the principal place of business of the Dutch East India Trading Company during the 17th century and again briefly from 1811 to 1814. A light Arak originated there. See also: Arak and Arrak.

Beer: Evidence indicates that Egyptians drank this fermented grain-based alcoholic beverage over 10,000 years ago, Native Americans brewed it before Christopher Columbus arrived, African tribes made it from grass seeds or local grains such as millet, and Japanese made it from rice (sake).

Here in America, beer may have played a part in encouraging the Mayflower to land on Plymouth Rock instead of a bit farther down the coast. Some say would-be settlers were almost out of the brew. Early American colonial laws (1700s) encouraged beer brewing so that stronger alcoholic beverages could be avoided. Even George Washington regularly ordered London porter until 1776, when he began boycotting more than tea.

In England, Porters (named for London working class men who carried things) and Stouts (meaning "strong") were born during the rise of the Industrial Revolution and were blessed by the British government, which saw beer as a way of curtailing its citizens' usage of gin. In fact, taverns were often called Porterhouses and served big pieces of beef called Porterhouse steaks.

By Tom's day, beer was widely sold in bottles. Before 1850, however, it wasn't. If you wanted to drink beer in the privacy of your own home, you could take a bucket or pot to your local tavern and they'd fill it up for you.

In the tavern, beer was sold in pints and quarts. Unruly patrons were told to "mind their pints and quarts," which is where we get the phrase "mind your ps and qs."

Benedictine: Can a group of people keep a secret for hundreds of years? They can when they are Benedictine monks. Since 1510, residents at the Fecamp, France monastery have kept the formula for their sweet liqueur "hush hush." What isn't secret, however, is their dedication. Each bottle bears the motto "Deo Optima Maximo" meaning "to God, most Good and most Great."

Bevo: By 1916, Tom Bullock's fellow St. Louis resident and most-famous brewer, August A. Busch, Sr., had anticipated Prohibition and developed a number of non-alcoholic products that would keep the company his father-in-law founded (now called Anheuser-Busch) financially solvent and workers employed. The best known of these is Bevo, a non-alcoholic beer that became an international phenomenon, selling in 20 countries.

"Bevo" is an English corruption "pivo," the Czechoslovakian and Slovakian word for beer. Pictured, a 10 fluid ounce bottle of Bevo was easy to distinguish from alcoholic beers. The colorful label features an eagle and a stork, and the bottle crown (not seen) pictured Reynard the witty fox from folklore, a symbol of Busch's cunningness.

Art courtesy of Anheuser-Busch, Inc.

With his recipe "Golfer's Delight - Home of Bevo - 18th Hole," Tom Bullock honors August Busch, a member of the St. Louis Country Club where Tom worked,

Bitters: Bitters got its name because, well, it's bitter and could take some of the sweetness out of mixed drinks.

Most often, Tom Bullock called for Angostura bitters, invented by a German military physician, Dr. Johann Siegert, in 1824, when in the city of Angostura, Venezuela. Ingredients include cascarilla, quasia, gentian, orange, quinine and other flavoring agents by infusion or distillation, but not Angostura bark, as some people say.

Tom Bullock, like other master bartenders of his time, used various bitters to enhance the flavor of the drinks he prepared. Popular with Tom, through World War I and the Roaring '20s, but difficult to find today is **Orange Bitters** made from the rind of sour or unripe oranges. See also: Calisaya.

Blackthorne: The Blackthorne Cocktail [sic] and Blackthorne Sour get their names from one of the ingredients, sloe gin. Sloe gin is flavored by the sloe plum, the fruit of the blackthorn tree.

Bourbon: Bourbon is the true song of the South and has probably inspired more music than any other whiskey. Story goes this American classic was born in Bourbon County, Tennessee, sometime around 1800 when Baptist minister Elijah Craig tried to save a little money. He cleaned an old oak barrel by singeing it with fire and then re-used the barrell to age whiskey. In 1855, a kid named Jack Daniels bought the minister's whiskey company and simulated the smooth taste by using a charcoal filter.

Brandy: Tom Bullock used many types of brandy (from the Dutch word meaning "burnt wine" because of the way it's distilled) in his drinks, including those made from fermented fruit. Old Brandy, such as that Tom used in a Brandy Scaffa, has been aged at least six years.

Brandy Roller Glass: A Brandy Snifter.

Bronx Cocktail: The Bronx Cocktail was invented during Tom Bullock's era by another master bartender, Johnnie Solon, at New York's old Waldorf Bar and became the Waldorf-Astoria's signature drink. Famous patrons known to imbibe there include

Ad from Life *magazine,*
June 19, 1913.

J. Pierpont Morgan, John W. "Bet-a-Million" Gates, Buffalo Bill Cody, and Mark Twain.

Burnette's Old Time Gin: See: Gin

Cacao: Cacao, according to the Aztecs, who drank it from gold goblets, came from heaven and consuming it imparts wisdom.

Calamus: Root of an herb called "Sweet Flag." It's said to have medicinal properties and a nice flavor and aroma.

Calisaya: Calisaya, from the bark of the Cinchona tree, was used as a medicinal tonic and was one of the principal sources for quinine in the late 1800s. According to the *American Journal of Pharmacy*, January, 1859, the preferred formula for mixing a Cordial Elixir of Calisaya included: calisaya bark, fresh orange peel, cinnamon, coriander, fennel, caraway, cardamon, cochineal and brandy. After distillation, it was mixed with a simple sugar syrup. Bartenders often bought the quinine tonic and mixed it with seltzer to become "tonic water" or "quinine water." It is now known simply as tonic.

Catawba: A Native American tribe and their language, a river running through North and South Carolina, a purplish wild grape, and the wine made from it.

Champagne: Tom Bullock may have sometimes used the term "Champagne" as many people do, to refer to any sparkling wine, even though it should only be used to refer to that from France's most northern wine growing region.

In turn of the 19th century America, sparkling wines were the rage, just as they had been in France and England since the 17th century, when a Benedictine monk named Dom Perignon (1638-1715) invented advances in fermentation and was the first vintner to press white wine from red grapes.

Claret: A light red wine, preferably a Bordeaux.

Club Soda: Carbon dioxide-charged water, also known as carbonated water. Similar to Sparkling Water, except the latter gets its bubbles naturally. See also: Seltzer.

Cobbler: This drink is reported to have been born in the U.S.A. and dates back to at least 1809 when Washington Irving (1783-1859), best remembered for writing *Rip Van Winkle,* mentioned it in his *History of New York.*

During Tom Bullock's era, the Cobbler was sherry or wine based and included pineapple syrup and various fresh fruit garnishes. During the 20th century, cobblers became liquor based.

Cocktail: Although alcoholic beverages have been mixed with other ingredients since antiquity, the Cocktail is an American phenomenon and the symbol of the high life throughout the modern world. The origination of the word is uncertain but some of the possibilities include:

1) Coquetier, from the French for eggcup, which was reportedly used to mix a drink in New Orleans sometime around 1800

2) Coquetel, the name of a mixed drink enjoyed by French officers during the American Revolution

3) Xochitl, an Aztec princess who supposedly seduced a king with a mixed drink

4) Cock Ale, a drink made from ale and a boiled fowl, dating back to the mid 1600s in England

5) Cock Ale, a mixture of spirits and other ingredients supposedly fed to cocks in order to anger them into fighting each other

6) Cock tailing, a practice of throwing a tailing of various left-over liquors together into the same receptacle and selling them at a lower price

7) A toast to the cock with the most feathers left in its tail after a fight by thirsty spectators after the event.

8) From the story of a saucy Elmsford, New York bar maid named Betsy Flanagan, who decorated her bar with cock feathers. One of her patrons asked for "one of those cock tails" and she delivered it in his glass

9) A horse with a docked tail that "cocks up" in front of a stage-coach

No matter where the name comes from, the cocktail, an alcoholic mixture with two or more ingredients, remains, according to H. L.

Mencken (1880-1956), the only American invention "... as perfect as the sonnet."

Cognac: A lovely Brandy, dating back to the 17th century, from the Bordeaux district in France. During Tom Bullock's day, only the wealthy could afford Cognac.

Collins: The Collins, a lemony drink similar to the Fizz and the Sour, may have been invented by Tom Collins at the Planter's Hotel in St. Louis as some say, or it may have been invented by John Collins, a waiter in England (who used Old Tom Gin, giving it its name).

Cooler: Especially in the years before air-conditioners, coolers helped soothe heat-conscious Southerners. All coolers have in common Ginger Ale, Club Soda or another type of carbonated beverage and the rind of a lemon or an orange cut in a continuous spiral with one end hooked over the rim of a tall glass.

Cordial: This name for a sweetened liqueur comes from the Latin, "Cor" or heart.

Corpse Reviver: Hangover "cures" probably came into existence right after the first hangover, but colorfully named Corpse Revivers were popular as far back as the late 1800s.

Creme de: The rich liqueurs used today don't usually contain cream. Tom Bullock used:

- Creme de Cocoa - a cocoa and vanilla liqueur, available in white and brown
- Creme de Menthe - the green, white, or clear versions taste like peppermint
- Creme de Noisette - a hazelnut liqueur
- Creme de Noyeau or Creme de Noya - flavored with bitter almonds
- Creme de Yvette or Creme de Violette - purplish liqueurs with a violet flavor. This liquor was named after French actress Yvette Gilbert

Crusta: A Crusta is usually a short sour drink served in a glass lined with sugar and an orange or lemon peel cut in a continuous strip, but variations abound. This thirst quencher may have been invented to counter New Orleans' heat and humidity in the mid-1800s by the owner of Santini's Saloon.

Cup: A punch drink made for one and by the glass instead of in a bowl for parties.

Curacao: Seventeenth century sailors didn't get enough vitamin C in their diet and came down with scurvy, among other things. Curacao, a liqueur made from dried orange peel, spirits, and rum was invented by the Dutch on the island of Curacao, off the coast of Venezuela. The concoction didn't actually help against scurvy, but suffering sailors did seem a little happier.

Varieties of Curacao made with cognac include Cointreau and Grand Marnier. Triple Sec may be substituted for red Curacao.

Cusiner Grenadine: See: Grenadine.

Daisy: In the 1850s, early versions of the Daisy were served without ice and in an iced metal mug, but by Tom Bullock's day this large drink was served in a goblet. Today, Daisies are usually served in a highball glass.

Dash: A splash of liquid. If you really need to measure, use 1/3 of a barspoon or 1/6th of a teaspoon measurement.

Drachm: Also called a dram, meaning "a small drink." A drachm measures about 1/16th of an ounce.

Eggs: Many of Tom Bullock's drink recipes call for raw eggs. While that may not have caused concern in 1917, it may today because there have been several salmonella-related food poisonings reported, primarily because of mishandling. If you have a weakened immune system or are concerned, use a pasteurized egg substitute from your grocery store.

Eggnogs: Famous mid-19th century bartender Jerry Thomas invented this cousin of the flip (which has the eggs but not the cream) for any occasion, but now it's most often served warm and at Christmas and New Year's Eve.

Fifty-Fifty: Tom Bullock's way of reminding you the quantity of the ingredients he's talking about should be equal.

Fish House Punch: Supposedly this was one of George Washington's favorite drinks. It's said to come from the State in Schuylkill Club, founded in 1732 in Philadelphia.

Fizz: When the old siphon bottle infused a stream of bubbles into this drink it made a "fizz" sound that gave this drink its name. A Fizz is a Sour (lemon juice, sugar, liquor) shaken and then infused with Club Soda or Seltzer Water.

Flip: Some say Ben Franklin invented the Rum Flip to celebrate victory at the Boston Tea Party when he placed a red-hot fireplace poker (called "flip iron" or "flip dog") into the cup and stirred it. The recipe for flips hasn't changed much in over 200 years although now we don't use a red-hot fireplace poker to warm our drinks. During the revolutionary war, folks loved Flips and drank them hot or cold.

Float: To carefully pour one liqueur over another so that one sits on top without being mixed, as in a pousse.

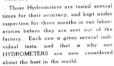

Alcohol Spirit Proof Testers

Will tell you the amount of alcohol in any liquid form from 1 to 200 proof

U. S. Government Hydrometer

Used by the Custom House

DIRECTIONS. Place liquid to be tested in one of our TESTING JARS, insert one of our HYDROMETERS in it as per our print on the right. The higher the "PROOF" the lower the Hydrometer will sink. Should it sink until the letter P is reached you have 100 "PROOF," or at 90 above P, 190 "PROOF," or at 80, below P, then you have 20 "PROOF," etc.

These Hydrometers are tested several times for their accuracy, and kept under inspection for three months in our laboratories before they are sent out of the factory. Each one is given several individual tests, and that is why our HYDROMETERS are now considered about the best in the world.

To get an accurate reading it is necessary to have the liquid tested at a temperature of 60 degrees F.

PRICES

TESTER 50c
JAR 50c

17

During Prohibition, alcohol was illegal to drink but not, apparently, to test.

Ad from the 1920 United Beverage Company catalog.

Gibson: Tom Bullock called this drink a Gibson Cocktail, but it was identical to the Martini of his day. This pre-Prohibition classic was probably named after Charles Dana Gibson (1867-1944) who sketched the lovely young Gibson Girls of the 1890s.

Gill: (pronounced "Jill") An old-fashioned measurement of 1/2 cup or 4 fluid ounces.

Gin: In 1650, the plight of sailors suffering from tropical diseases inspired the world of medicine to make yet another contribution to modern revelry. Dutch professor of medicine Franciscus de la Boe (also known as Franciscus Sylvius) developed a concoction from the herb juniper (in Dutch called jenever, in French called genievre, and soon shortened to Gin) that helped fight fever and serve as a diuretic.

Gin immigrated to the United States with the first Dutch settlers, but didn't become a booming success until Prohibition, when it became the most consumed liquor. Because Gin was so easy and inexpensive to make, drinking it became the rage of its age. From a taste point of view, however, Gin left something to be savored. Mixed drink "Cocktails" contained sweeteners and other flavorings that hid the taste of bad Gin.

Use these modern translations to choose the Gins most similar to the ones Tom Bullock used:

- Dry Gin is unsweetened Gin. Now the term is outmoded because all gins are dry except Old Tom Gin.

- Old Tom Gin is a sweetened Gin popular between 1700-1900. Tom Bullock used it in many recipes, but it's very difficult to find outside of England.

- London Dry Gin is an unsweetened Gin.

- Plym or Plymouth Gin is a type of Gin made in Plymouth, England that is aromatic and slightly sweeter than London Gin.

- Gordon's Gin: Bullock calls for this Gin by name in many of his recipes. It's still available and is a London Dry Gin.

Gin is still considered by many to be one of the most fundamental liquors for mixed drinks.

Grenadine: Grenadine was one of Tom Bullock's favorite flavoring syrups. In 1900, Grenadine was made from the juice and pulp of pomegranates and was so sweet only a few drops were needed. Granada, the Caribbean island where the pomegranates were grown, still gives the flavoring its name even though it's now made from red currants. Add extra Grenadine or other sweetener to Tom's recipes to accommodate your taste.

Gum Syrup: See syrup.

Highball: A highball is usually liquor, Club Soda, and any flavoring in a large glass over ice. Some say the Highball got its name from a railroad sign (a ball raised high on a pole) meaning "Full Speed Ahead." Others say it received that name because it's so fast to assemble. Still others say the word "ball" is bartender slang for a glass.

Ice: Ice is usually the first ingredient Tom Bullock specified in a recipe because of its importance to the taste of the drink.

During most of Tom's life, ice was a luxury. Until he was about 20 years old, ice had to be cut from frozen lakes in winter, hauled ashore, cut into blocks, and kept in cold storage. Tom probably ordered his ice from an ice man, stored it in an ice box, and shaved, cracked, lamped, pieced, or smashed it into smaller pieces by hand. Refrigerators weren't available until a year before Tom Bullock's 1917 book came out and were expensive ... about $900.00, the price of a new car.

Julep: The Julep may be among the oldest drinks in the world, but it took America (and American liquor) to make it a classic.

Some say the word comes from Persian (julâb) for "rosewater." H. L. Mencken thinks the word came into English in about 1400 from the Spanish and Portuguese by way of the French (julepe). One thing is certain: a Brandy Julep is mentioned in America around 1809, many years before Kentucky Bourbon was born.

In Tom Bullock's day, Juleps were always served in a chilled silver or pewter tankard. Now the sweet delight is traditionally served the first Saturday in May at the Kentucky Derby and any other time relief from southern heat and humidity mandates.

Aficionados agree that the secret of a Julep is good, fresh mint, but fight over whether or not to muddle the leaves. Master bartender and southern son Tom Bullock muddled in some recipes and not in others.

Kuemmel or Kummel: A liqueur flavored with anise, caraway seeds, and other herbs, created in Holland but now made in Germany, too.

Lillet: A popular French wine-based aperitif.

Liqueurs: These ancient marvels pack a little more power than the average herb or spice does alone. Most liqueurs were originally concocted as medicines, but have evolved into sweetened indulgences sure to be enjoyed straight up or mixed into a cocktail. See also: Cordial.

Loaf Sugar: In 1900, store-bought sugar was often pressed into a cloth bag. The bag was "loaf" shaped, larger at the bottom and tapered to an open top.

Lump Sugar: Sugar pressed into cubes.

Madeira: Fortified wine from the Portuguese island of Madeira. Used as a dessert wine or for cooking.

Manhattan: How would you like it if someone named a drink in honor of your mother? Winston Churchill didn't seem to mind.

In 1874, before Jennie Jerome (1854-1921) crossed the big pond and married Churchill's father, she gave a party for the new governor of New York at the big apple's famous Manhattan Club. The bartender commemorated the event by serving the first Manhattan. Later, Jennie is credited with saying, "You may be a princess or the richest woman in the world, but you cannot be more than a lady."

Maraschino: Maraschino is a liqueur made from the fermented juice of marasca, a sour cherry from Dalmatia. Dalmatia is now part of present day Yugoslavia, near the Adriatic sea. See also the recipe for: Crimean Cup A La Marmora.

Marsala: Marsala, a port city in Sicily, has been famous for making fortified wines like Marsala since Roman times. See: Port.

Martini: Nikita Khrushchev (1894-1971) called the Martini "America's lethal weapon" and he's rumored to have known.

The Martini may be the "King of Cocktails" but even though the Hueblein Company offered a pre-mixed Martini as early as 1894, the Martini didn't become really popular until Prohibition.

At the core of this cocktail are Vermouth and Gin, although the ratio has changed dramatically over the years. The perfect Martini in the 1880s had about equal parts of Gin to Vermouth. One-hundred years later, the Vermouth has almost disappeared. In fact, Winston Churchill said he made a Martini by pouring Gin while he glanced at an unopened Vermouth bottle.

"GET ME OUT OF THIS WET COAT AND INTO A DRY MARTINI!"

ROBERT BENCHLEY (1889-1945)

Measurements: Master bartenders like Tom Bullock are so experienced they usually don't have to measure. Here's a translation for the rest of us:

- gill – 4 fluid ounces or 1/2 cup
- jigger – 1 1/2 ounce shot glass
- lemon – 1 medium yields about 3 tablespoons of juice
- orange – 1 medium yields about 1/3 cup of juice
- pony – 1 ounce
- sugar – 1 pound of granulated sugar = about 2 1/2 cups
- wine glass – 4 ounces

Moselle: A light, dry white wine produced in the valley of the Moselle River.

Muddler: A mortar or rod with a broad, rounded or flattened end used to grind ingredients.

Old Fashion: Mr. Tom Bullock called it an Old Fashion, today we call it an Old Fashioned. This American classic is said to have been invented at Tom's alma mater, the Pendennis Club in Louisville, Kentucky.

Onion: Refers to a cocktail onion, which is a small pearl onion cooked and/or pickled.

Onion Cocktail: Tom Bullock called this drink an Onion Cocktail, but now we call it a Gibson. And what Tom called a Gibson, we now call a Martini.

Orgeat: An almond flavored syrup or cordial. See: Syrup.

Pewter Mug: Mugs made from pewter and silver were common before the 19th century, when technological advances in glass-making made drinking out of glassware more practical. By the time Tom Bullock tended bar, pewter and silver mugs were cherished for their history, just as we might use an antique champange flute to make a wedding toast.

Planter's Punch: The founder of Meyer's Rum is credited with inventing Planter's Punch in the 1800s, as is Tom Collins, the bartender at the Planter's Hotel in St. Louis in 1858. Sometimes Tom Collins is also said to have invented the drink that bears his name. See: Punches.

Pony: A pony is a small horse, so it only makes sense a pony drink would be a small one ... about 2/3rds of a jigger or 1 ounce. Don't be surprised if the bartender asks you to "pony up" when it's time to pay ... the word has worked its way deep into our vocabulary.

Pony Glass: A small stemmed glass holding 1 to 2 ounces of liquid. See also: Pony.

Pony glass

Illustration courtesy Steve Quinn

Port: Necessity is the mother of invention, and when it comes to brandy, Port is one really fine drink. Seafarers shipping out of Oporto, Portugal, in the 17th century needed two things: 1) a way to economically carry wines, which were taking up too much valuable cargo space, and 2) a way to make wines last longer. Someone got the idea that they could boil the water out of the wine and add it back in when they got to the next port. Then another entrepreneur tasted it and liked it better than the brandy! A sweet fortified wine called Port was born.

Pousse-cafe: Translated from the French, Pousse-cafe means, literally, "push back the coffee." These spectacularly layered after-dinner drinks, created in New Orleans around 1850, inspired turn-of-the-century Americans to postpone their coffee in droves!

Only the most patient and experienced bartenders learn how to pour a pousse-cafe so that the different liqueurs lie on top of each other without mixing. Drinking a pousse is a luxury even today as pleasure-seekers who know sip through each of 2 to 7 layers, one at a time.

Pousse Glass: A small stemmed glass used for Pousse-cafes. The glasses have straight sides, so that the liqueurs can be more easily balanced.

Behind Tom Bullock's Bar

Powdered Sugar: WARNING: When Tom Bullock — or another from his time — calls for powdered sugar, he is referring to fine or superfine granulated sugar, not confectioner's sugar.

Prohibition: Fifty years after the Prohibition Party was founded and over two years after Tom Bullock published *The Ideal Bartender,* the 18th Amendment to the Constitution was ratified by 36 states and the bars finally closed.

Liquor consumption exploded and the legislation proved to be a complete disaster as Americans drank with a vengeance. As Spanish film maker Luis Brunmel says in his 1982 memoirs, "I never drank so much in my life as the time I spent five months in the United States during Prohibition."

Franklin Delano Roosevelt enthusiastically celebrated the end of Prohibition in 1934 by stirring up a big batch of Martinis. He is reported to have been a better president than mixologist.

Punches: Making punch drinks for wedding receptions, ladies' luncheons, and large celebrations would have been a big part of Tom Bullock's job at the St. Louis Country Club. He lists over 26 delicious punch recipes in *The Ideal Bartender,* and we've included all of them here.

Some believe the word "punch" comes from the Hindu word "Panch" or "Pantsh" meaning 5, because 5 or more ingredients are included in most punch recipes. Others believe the word is shortened from "Puncheon" a small cask holding about 80 gallons of liquid, from which sailors drank communally.

Ramos Gin Fizz: A classic even in Tom Bullock's era. The Ramos Gin Fizz was invented in the late 1800s by celebrated New Orleans bartender Harry C. Ramos.

Rickey: The Rickey was named for Colonel Joe Rickey, a Washington lobbyist in the late 1800s. The refreshing drink is usually made with gin, lime juice, Club Soda, and ice. A true Rickey contains no sugar or sweetener. That lack of sweetness is not meant to cast aspersions on the good Colonel, who was known to be something of a drinker, especially at Washington, D.C.'s Shoemaker's restaurant.

Rock Candy: A candy made by letting concentrated sugar-water dry and harden over several days as the water evaporates. Rock Candy swizzle sticks like Tom Bullock made for customers are easy and fun to make. Just boil 1 cup of water, let cool, add 2 cups of sugar and stir until dissolved. Reheat water and slowly add as much sugar as will disappear. Let the syrup cool and, as it does, dip wooden stir sticks into the mixture and let dry overnight. Redip and dry as desired. See: Syrup.

Rum: In the late 1700s, Colonists drank Rum because it was cheap and plentiful. By 1900, when Tom Bullock was tending bar, Rum was more often thought of as something poor people drank, although Tom used it in many delightful drinks and punches for his wealthy clients.

When the recipe specifies Jamaican Rum, try a dark one.

Rye: Immigrants, especially those from Germany and Northern Ireland, were not familiar with Native American corn when they came to the United States and were hesitant to use the strange yellow vegetable as an ingredient in their recipes. They began making whiskey out of rye in the 1700s, and Rye whiskey remained a popular drink through the 1950s.

Sangaree: A tall drink containing chilled spirits, wine or beer, and sometimes dusted with grated nutmeg. Sangaree was popular in the mid-18th century. It borrows its name from the Spanish Sangria (meaning blood), and is equally delicious served hot or cold.

Sarsaparilla: Tom Bullock and his contemporaries incorrectly believed bottled Sarsaparilla (from the Spanish for zarza, a bramble, and parilla, a little vine) had medicinal properties. Modern scientists say the plant from Central America may have health benefits, but the bottled soda pop Tom used didn't.

Seltzer: A naturally bubbly water named after the German town of its origin. In the late 1800s, we learned how to weave bubbles into water ourselves and have been manufacturing a Seltzer knock-off ever since. One of the advantages of Seltzer is that the sodium bicarbonate ingredient helps soothe acidic stomachs. See also: Club Soda.

Short Glass: A "short glass" contains 2 to 3 ounces.

Shrub: Shrubs originated in merry old England. They're made by soaking fruits in spirits for a week or more and bottling them. For the kiddies or alcohol conscious, non-alcoholic shrubs can be made from fruit juice, vinegar, and sugar and are OK to drink right after mixing.

Smash: The Smash gets its name from the ice, which was smashed fine from an ice block with a utensil.

Soda: Originally a health drink served by pharmacists. Before truth in advertising, many soda waters claimed to cure all ails.

Sour Glass: Stemmed glass that holds 5 to 6 ounces.

Advertisement from
The Modern Priscilla, 1894.

Sugar: See Bar Sugar, Loaf Sugar, Lump Sugar, Powdered Sugar.

Syrup: Mr. Bullock called for Gum Syrup in many drinks, probably because crystallized sugar doesn't mix well in alcohol. Mr. Bullock often used the French spelling (Sirop) instead of the American spelling in his recipes. Gum Syrup is also called sugar syrup, gomme syrup, or, more often today, simple sugar.

Great flavored syrups are on the market today, but it's easy to make one. For Gum Syrup, just add 1 part sugar to 2 parts water, bring to a boil, bottle, and refrigerate. To make a fruit syrup, substitute 1 part sugar to 2 parts juice, depending on the sweetness of the fruit.

In Tom's time, Orgeat syrup was a blend of barley and almonds. Now it contains almonds, sugar, and rosewater or orange flower water.

One ounce of Vodka to every ten ounces of syrup will act as a preservative. See: Orgeat.

Tall Glass: A glass containing 5 or more ounces.

Toddy: Toddies were very popular between 1800 and 1860. Master bartenders like Tom Bullock heated this drink over an open fire or stove fueled with wood and knew never to actually bring the alcohol to a boil.

Tokay: This Hungarian delight was once known as the "Wine of Kings."

Tom & Jerry: Famous bartender Jerry Thomas invented the Tom & Jerry, a cousin of the flip, and named it after himself in the mid-1800s.

Vermouth: Some believe Vermouth was invented soon after wine by an ancient medicine man who added healing herbs to the wine for curative reasons.

In Tom Bullock's day, sweet Vermouth came from Italy and dry Vermouth came from France. Now both come from either, but when the British say they want something served "French" they mean mixed with dry Vermouth.

Vermouth got its name from the German (Vermut) for wormwood, which, like Absinthe, it originally contained.

Vodka: Vodka was virtually unknown in the U.S. until the 1950s. One of our favorite drinks made with Vodka, the Bloody Mary, wasn't born until a few years after Tom Bullock wrote his book (in 1924 at Harry's Bar & American Grill, Paris).

Whiskey: Tom used the Irish spelling of the word "whiskey" throughout this book and it seems the Irish deserve the honor. Evidence suggests they have been distilling the brew for over 900 years and their word for the brew originally meant "water of life."

Ad in *Leslie's Weekly,*
September 25, 1902.

Scotch and Canadian Whisky can be easily discerned on your shelf because the word is spelled without the "e."

Most American Whiskey is made in Kentucky because that area was open frontier land in 1794, when the government levied taxes on whiskey production to pay off American Revolution debts. Whiskey producers moved west to Kentucky to avoid paying taxes.

Consumption of whiskey soared during the westward movement of the United States because whiskey was portable and durable. Unlike wine or beer, whiskey could be carried in a flask for hundreds of miles over rough terrain without spoiling.

Whiskey Glass: Also known as an Old-fashioned or Rocks Glass (4 to 8 ounce).

Wine: People have been enjoying wine for at least four thousand years. Wine jars dating from before 1700 B.C. were discovered in the Delta of Egypt, and clay jars with stoppers and wine residue were discovered in the tombs of pharaohs. In about the 5th century B.C. Greek historian Herodotus mentions shipping wine down the Euphrates or Tigris to Babylon. A fermented beverage of wine, barley beer, and honey mead was served at King Midas' funerary feast.

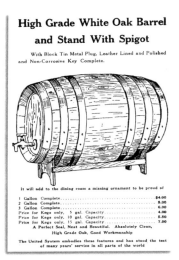

High Grade White Oak Barrel and Stand With Spigot

With Block Tin Metal Plug, Leather Lined and Polished and Non-Corrosive Key Complete.

It will add to the dining room a missing ornament to be proud of

1 Gallon Complete	$4.00
2 Gallon Complete	5.00
3 Gallon Complete	6.00
Price for Kegs only, 5 gal. Capacity	4.00
Price for Kegs only, 10 gal. Capacity	5.50
Price for Kegs only, 15 gal. Capacity	7.00

A Perfect Seal, Neat and Beautiful. Absolutely Clean, High Grade Oak, Good Workmanship

The United System embodies these features and has stood the test of many years' service in all parts of the world

Product offered by the United Beverage Company catalog in 1921.

Tom Bullock used a number of varieties of wine including Angelica, Catawba (also known as Sweet Catawba), Chateau Margaux, Claret, Madeira, and Moselle.

Wine Glass: About 4 ounces.

Worcestershire Sauce: Legend has it, in the 1840s a barrel of spice vinegar was forgotten and began to ferment in a Worcestershire chemist's shop. Someone tasted it before throwing it out and the rest is history.

Before Prohibition, libations were poured in rocking hotel, dining, or private railroad cars by men like Tom Bullock whose title may have been "Conductor" or "Porter" but who also tended bar. If the train careened through "dry" counties or states, it was this man's duty to remove all traces of alcohol. In "wet" counties, it was also this man's duty to track each drink he poured and collect any taxes due.

Denver and Rio Grande Railroad beverage menu from 1905 courtesy of Harry Bilger.

BEVERAGE INDEX

* Indicates a non-alcoholic drink

> "THE ONLY THINGS THAT THE
> UNITED STATES HAS GIVEN TO THE WORLD
> ARE SKYSCRAPERS, JAZZ, AND COCKTAILS.
> THAT IS ALL."
>
> FEDERICO GARCÍA LORCA (1898–1936)

Index

From Germany, 1886

RESOURCES

Berry Bros. & Rudd
(hard-to-find wines & Absinthe)
3 St. James's St.
London, SW1A 1EG
Telephone: 0870 900 4300
Fax: 0870 900 4301
www.bbr.com

K & L Wine Merchants
(hard-to-find wines)
Telephone: 800-247-5987
Fax: 650-364-4687
klwines.com

Laird & Company
(Applejack)
One Laird Road
Scobeyville, NJ 07724
Telephone: 877-438-5247
Facsimile: 732-542-2244
www.LAIRDANDCOMPANY.com

Laytons Wine Merchants Limited
(hard-to-find wines & Absinthe)
20 Midland Road
London NW1 2AD
Telephone: 020 7388 4567
Facsimile: 020 7383 7419
www.laytons.co.uk

Routin America, Inc.
(syrups)
PO Box 460003
Glendale, CO 80246
Telephone : 303-300-0400
Fax : 303-300-0500
e mail: routinusa@aol.com
www.routin.com and www.1883.com

Sam's Wines & Spirits
(hard-to-find wines & spirits)
1720 N. Marcey St.
Chicago, IL 60614
Telephone: 1-800-777-9137
www.samswine.com

Torani
(syrups)
223 East Harris Avenue
South San Francisco, CA 94080
Telephone: 800-775-1925
www.torani.com

THE USUAL DISCLAIMERS

The recipes in this book have all been excerpted from Tom Bullock's 1917 cocktail book, *The Ideal Bartender*. They are not guaranteed, although the ones we've tried (and tried again) are absolutely delicious. Still, we beg you:

1) Don't drink in excess   2) Don't drink and drive

And the editors, authors, and publisher of this book hope Mr. Bullock has given you at least 173 reasons to stay home!

Space was at a premium on railroad cars, so wine cellars were built into a wall at one end of a train car or into a chest under the floor. This 1901 dining car menu is from the Oregon Railroad and Navigation Company, a Union Pacific predecessor.

Menu courtesy of Harry Bilger.

The Southwest Limited
Kansas City—Excelsior Springs—Chicago

DINNER

COEURS

OLIVES   LETTUCE WITH EGG   CELERY

GREEN TURTLE, MADEIRA   CONSOMME, PRINTANIER

BOILED MACKEREL,
BAYONNE SAUCE

POTTED SQUAB
BORDELAISE

ROAST PRIME BEEF   SPRING LAMB
NATURAL   MINT SAUCE

NEW POTATOES IN CREAM   CAULIFLOWER AU GRATIN
SUMMER SQUASH   NEW ASPARAGUS

COMBINATION SALAD
FRENCH DRESSING

RHUBARB PIE   STRAWBERRY SOUFFLE

ICE CREAM   ASSORTED CAKE

CAMEMBERT, EDAM, ROQUEFORT AND WAUKESHA CREAM CHEESE
BENT'S WATER CRACKERS, TOASTED

COFFEE   TEA

DINNER ONE DOLLAR

April 7, 1912

WINE LIST

CHAMPAGNE

CLARETS

WHITE WINES

BURGUNDIES

RHINE WINE

CALIFORNIA WINE ASSOCIATION'S "CALWA" BRAND

GUNDLACH-BUNDSCHU WINE CO. WINES

ITALIAN SWISS COLONY

CORDIALS, LIQUORS, ETC.

CIGARS

Easter of 1912 inspired the Chicago, Milwaukee & St. Paul Railroad to
create a special menu for their "Southwest Limited" train. For the grand
sum of $1.00, travelers between Kansas City and Chicago could procure
a feast. For $2.25, they could choose among The Southwest Limited's
finest champagnes. Cocktails were available for 20 cents each.

Menu courtesy of Harry Bilger.

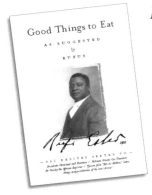